RTI: Easy Phonics Interventions

by Kama Einhorn

NEW YORK • TORONTO • LONDON • AUCKLAND • SYDNEY
MEXICO CITY • NEW DELHI • HONG KONG • BUENOS AIRES

Teaching Resources

For Lily

and Nina Monaco

This book could not have been written without the valuable frameworks
and foundations provided by Wiley Blevins in *Phonics From A to Z: A Practical Guide*
and Brenda M. Weaver, Ed.D., in *RTI: Assessments & Remediation for K–2.*

Edited by Immacula A. Rhodes
Cover design by Brian LaRossa
Interior design by Kathy Massaro

ISBN: 978-0-545-23696-6

Text copyright © 2011 by Kama Einhorn
Illustrations © 2011 by Scholastic Inc.
Illustrations by Teresa Anderko, Maxie Chambliss, Rusty Fletcher, James Graham Hale, and Anne Kennedy.
All rights reserved. Published by Scholastic Inc.
Printed in the U.S.A.

1 2 3 4 5 6 7 8 9 10   40   18 17 16 15 14 13 12 11

Contents

Introduction 4

Using This Book 5

Connections to the Language Arts Standards ... 7

Recommended Timing & Dosage 8

Multisensory Activities 9

References 10

Skills-Tracker Chart 11

Weekly Lessons

Short Vowels (CVC)

Week 1

a 13

a 15

e 17

e 19

Week 2

i 21

i 23

o 25

u 27

Long Vowel Digraphs & Silent *e* (CVC*e*)

Week 3

ai 29

ay 31

ea 33

ee 35

Week 4

oa 37

silent *e* (a_e) 39

silent *e* (i_e) 41

silent *e* (o_e, u_e) 43

Variant Vowels & Diphthongs

Week 5

ar 45

aw 47

oo (as in *moon*) 49

oo (as in *book*) 51

Week 6

oi 53

ou 55

ow 57

oy 59

Consonant Blends & Digraphs

Week 7

br 61

cl 63

cr 65

fl 67

Week 8

gr 69

sl 71

st 73

tr 75

Week 9

ch 77

sh 79

th 81

wh 83

Word Families

Week 10

-ack 85

-ell 87

-est 89

-ick 91

Week 11

-ill 93

-ink 95

-ock 97

-ump 99

Early Structural Analysis: Prefixes & Suffixes

Week 12

re- 101

un- 103

-ed 105

-ing 107

Answers 109

Introduction

What Is RTI?

RTI, or Response to Intervention, has come to the forefront of literacy instruction in many states and school districts in the United States. The goal of the RTI model is for teachers to assess student progress in all areas of literacy, to provide early, effective and appropriate interventions, and to determine when to refer students for evaluation of suspected specific learning disabilities.

RTI is implemented differently across states and districts, but the key elements of any RTI approach are:

* using research-based instruction and interventions in the classroom

* monitoring and measuring student progress in response to that instruction and intervention

* using assessment data to modify instruction so it meets students' needs

Of course, you are likely already helping your students succeed by simply and instinctually adjusting your teaching to accommodate individual children's needs. All teachers who are helping struggling children learn are practicing RTI in some form by following the basic sequence of "teach the skill, assess whether it has been learned, and intervene when necessary." The current version of RTI is new because, at a policy level, it mandates research-based instructional practices and progress monitoring. In addition, RTI offers a measurable way to help all children "reach, at a minimum, proficiency on challenging state academic standards and state academic assessments" as mandated by the No Child Left Behind Act of 2001.

Most RTI programs include three tiers: regular classroom instruction with regular assessments (tier 1), targeted interventions (tier 2), and evaluation for specific learning disabilities (tier 3). This book focuses on tier 2, the "targeted intervention"—or remediation—phase of the RTI model. In *Assessments & Remediation for K–2* (Scholastic, 2009), Brenda M. Weaver, Ed.D., describes tier 2:

> "The middle tier involves more intense and differentiated instruction for students identified as lagging behind their peers. [The tier] may include supplemental instruction provided by another professional, either in the classroom or in an outside setting. Each student's progress is monitored over a period of time using assessments…Reading specialists or literacy coaches…can offer support." (pp. 11–12)

The lessons in this resource, developed for second and third graders, cover many of the essential first grade phonics skills, as identified by Wiley Blevins in *Phonics From A to Z* (2006). Taken together, the lessons comprise a 12-week phonics intervention program, including recommended timing and dosage to help you gauge the areas in need of intervention, track student progress, and perform assessments to determine students' mastery of the content. If students continue to struggle after this intervention, you would then consider moving them to the final tier, at which they would be evaluated for possible inclusion in special education. The completed lesson pages and Skills-Tracker Chart serve as valuable tools when discussing students' progress with your school reading specialist, special education teacher, or literacy coach.

What Is Phonics and Why Focus on Early Phonics Intervention?

There are different elements of literacy—phonics, decoding, fluency, writing, comprehension, and vocabulary—all crucial pieces to completing the puzzle that is reading success. The pages in this book focus on the phonics piece of that puzzle. Phonics help readers map sounds into spellings, enabling them to decode words. Decoding is the manipulation and comprehension of spoken and written sounds.

It's critical to reach at-risk students with explicit phonics instruction before the end of third grade. Until third grade, students are focused on learning to read—recognizing letters and their sounds and decoding words. But everything shifts in third grade. At this level, students are expected to "read to learn." They should be spending less cognitive energy on decoding and exerting more on comprehending what they read. They must be able to read fluently enough to focus on the meaning of the text.

These early years are crucial for establishing a foundation for lifelong learning, creating motivated, confident readers and writers who know the joy of self-expression, the benefits of clear communication, and the delight in gleaning new knowledge.

By the end of second grade, children should be able to:

- Refine the use of the sound-symbol strategy in decoding (double vowels and phonetic clusters)

- Understand and apply affixes (prefixes and suffixes)

Using This Book

The 12 weekly lessons in this book include skill-building activities that teach and reinforce 48 phonics skills essential to rapid decoding success. The activities provide a balanced phonics lesson for each targeted skill and align with research-based best teaching practices. The phonics skills targeted in these lessons include:

❋ **Short Vowels:** Weeks 1 and 2 focus on the simple consonant-vowel-consonant (CVC) sound-spelling pattern, as in *cat* and *sit*. This is the most straightforward way to teach short vowel sounds.

❋ **Long Vowel Digraphs & Silent e:** Long vowel sounds in English can appear in a variety of ways. Weeks 3 and 4 explore the long vowel sounds in vowel digraphs (such as *ai* or *ay*, as in *rain* or *ray*) and the CVC*e* pattern (as in *cage, vine,* and *note*).

❊ **Variant Vowels & Diphthongs:** The English language is full of sound-spelling patterns that must simply be memorized and reinforced through exposure and repetition. Weeks 5 and 6 explore several common variant vowel combinations (such as *ar* in *star* and *oo* in *book*) and diphthongs (*ou* as in *house* and *oi* as in *coin*).

❊ **Consonant Blends & Digraphs:** Blends are combinations of letters in which each letter retains a separate sound (like *cr* as in *cry*). Weeks 7 and 8 focus on eight initial blends that students will encounter frequently in reading. Week 9 targets initial consonant digraphs—combinations of letters that create a different sound than that made by each individual letter (like *ch* as in *chip*). Explicit instruction of consonant digraphs helps students decode words more rapidly.

❊ **Word Families:** Also known as phonograms, word families are a great way to recognize common spelling patterns. For instance, words in the *-ack* family include *back, black, lack, pack, sack, tack,* and so on. Almost 500 primary-grade words can be derived from a very small set of word families. When students learn that words contain recognizable chunks that always sound the same, they've taken an important step on the road to reading fluency. Weeks 10 and 11 target several word families that students will encounter often.

❊ **Early Structural Analysis:** Students in second and third grade encounter a growing number of words that contain affixes. When they can quickly recognize prefixes and suffixes such as *re-, un-, -ed,* and *-ing,* students can more easily tackle these longer words; the lessons in Week 12 provide word analysis strategies to help students do just that.

What's in Each Lesson

The lessons follow a predictable, consistent format as described below. Students can complete the activities in small, teacher-guided groups. The exercises are also appropriate for one-on-one instruction or for extra practice at home. Simple, quick, and flexible, each lesson reinforces a particular phonics skill from several different angles, giving students multiple opportunities to "get it" and to succeed. The front of each lesson page contains activities that introduce and reinforce the phonics skill—its spelling and sound pattern. The back of the page takes learning to the next level with activities that let students put what they have learned into practice.

To prepare a lesson, simply make a double-sided copy of the activity page for each student.

❊ **Introduction:** Here's where the skill is explicitly introduced (with a word and corresponding picture). You'll want to directly state the relationship between the sound and the spelling that is the focus of the lesson (Blevins, 2006). Walk students through this section by reading the activity aloud.

Tip

At the beginning of the intervention, you might provide pocket-folders for students to decorate and use to store their completed pages.

You might write and display the target word and its sound on chart paper (for instance, when teaching short *a* on page 13, write *a* and *cat*). Then demonstrate how to orally blend the sounds in the word as you run your finger under each letter (*c, a, t*). Point out the picture named by the word and have students trace or color the target letter(s) on their page.

❊ **Fill-in-the-Blank:** In this section, students complete the word for each picture by filling in the target letter or sound. This activity helps students apply their understanding of the letter-sound relationship and provides just enough scaffolding to ensure success: It focuses on individual words, not sentences or connected text, and uses picture cues for additional support.

❊ **Word Path or Word Puzzle:** This self-checking activity, included in the activities for Weeks 1–11, offers students more scaffolded practice and another built-in opportunity for success.

❊ **Show What You Know!:** Students apply what they've learned in this section. Fill-in-the-blank sentences provide context for students to use in choosing the correct words to complete them. You'll notice that the sentences contain many high-frequency words, giving students the opportunity to read controlled text—connected text in which a high proportion of the words are decodable. This provides a direct connection between the phonics skills taught and actual reading (Adams, 1990; Taylor & Nosbush, 1983). It also allows students to focus better on the target skill, since they'll already be familiar with many of the words in the sentences. Depending on students' reading level, you might read the sentences aloud, then have students read the words in the word box independently to make their choices.

❊ **All Together Now:** Use this call-and-response chant to reinforce children's understanding of the target skill while building reading fluency, increasing reading rate, and introducing more connected text. Each chant features lots of sight words as well as key target words. First, read each line aloud as students follow along using their fingers to track the text. (You might copy the chant onto chart paper to demonstrate tracking.) Then read the student lines ("Group" and "ALL" parts) aloud and have children repeat them (echo reading). Finally, perform the entire chant by reading the "Leader" line yourself and having students read the "Group" and "ALL" lines. Repeated reading activities such as these

Connections to the Language Arts Standards

The activities in this book are designed to support you in meeting the following standards as outlined by Mid-continent Research for Education and Learning (McREL), an organization that collects and synthesizes national and state K–12 curriculum standards.

Reading

● Uses basic elements of phonetic analysis (letter/sound relationships, beginning consonants, vowel sounds, blends, and word patterns) to decode unknown words

● Uses basic elements of structural analysis (syllables and spelling patterns) to decode unknown words

● Understands level-appropriate sight words and vocabulary

Writing

● Uses phonics knowledge and conventions of spelling in writing (spells phonetically regular words, uses letter-sound relationships, spells basic short-vowel, long-vowel, r-controlled, and consonant-blend patterns)

Source: Kendall, J. S. & Marzano, R. J. (2004). *Content knowledge: A compendium of standards and benchmarks for K–12 education.* Aurora, CO: Mid-continent Research for Education and Learning. Online database: http://www.mcrel.org/standards-benchmarks/

chants help build automaticity and comprehension skills (Samuels, 1988). Once you have recited a chant several times, try switching roles to give students (either individually or as a group) a chance to be the leader.

❋ **Write It!:** Writing is a key component in any phonics lesson. This section helps students make a reading-writing connection and gives them the opportunity to use the targeted sound-spelling relationship in their own writing. Students can write their own sentences on the provided lines, or you might have students dictate each sentence to you as you write it on chart paper. Later, students can copy their sentence onto their paper. Once it is written out, have students read their sentence, saying each word aloud and tracking it with their finger. Encourage them to pay special attention to the target word. Have students read their sentence several times until they read it fluently and independently.

Recommended Timing & Dosage

Each state and district implements RTI differently, so there are many ways to bring this resource into your classroom. You can use the lessons in any way that best meets your students' needs. The following sequence is recommended:

❋ **Pre-Test:** Conduct formal and informal assessments at the beginning of the school year (or prior to implementing the lessons in this intervention program). These assessments, which can be found in *Phonics From A to Z* by Wiley Blevins (Scholastic, 2006), are helpful tools in identifying struggling or at-risk students who might benefit from tier 2 RTI phonics instruction:

- Checklist: Possible Characteristics of Student With Reading Problems (page 203)
- Nonsense Word Test (pages 196–197)
- San Diego Quick Assessment (LaPray & Ross, 1969) for elementary grades (page 198–199)

You might re-administer the assessments halfway through the intervention period to monitor student progress.

❋ **Intervention:** Begin the intervention with those students that have been identified as candidates who would benefit from extra instruction. The lessons take about 20 minutes a day and can be conducted with small groups or one-on-one with individual students. Each week's lesson includes four pages—one for each day from Monday through Thursday. (Fridays are set aside for review and weekly assessments.) Each day, students complete both the front and back of a different lesson page from the same week's lessons. The lessons let you teach one skill at a time—and teach it until it is "over-learned." You can adjust the pace at which you introduce skills, allowing students time to master each skill before moving on. The activities are designed to enable you to conduct a continuous review of students' progress as they apply what they know to real reading and writing in context.

✳ **Daily and Weekly Assessments:** Use the Skills-Tracker Chart (pages 11–12) to conduct both daily and weekly assessments. Copy a chart for each student and fill out the top of the chart. Assessments can be done with small groups or individuals.

- For daily assessments, ask students to put away the skill page they just completed. Then conduct a short dictation exercise by reading aloud five target words for students to write on a separate sheet of paper. (See the word list on the Skills-Tracker Chart for the designated day and week.) Students can correct their own papers for immediate feedback. Record assessment results on students' Skills-Tracker Charts.

- Give weekly assessments on Fridays. First, you might want to review the target skill(s) of the week. The multisensory activities (pages 9–10) are ideal for this purpose—just choose an activity and use words students worked with during the week in the activity. For the weekly assessment, conduct a short dictation exercise, similar to the daily assessments. You can use the list of ten words in the Skills-Tracker Chart for the assessment.

✳ **Post-Test:** At the end of the 12 weeks, administer the same assessments you used before the intervention. Share your assessment data along with students' lesson pages with your school's reading specialist, literacy coach, or special education teacher to help you determine what the next step might be for at-risk students.

Keep in mind that none of the suggested assessments can replace your own observations or informal assessments. Rather, they can add to them by providing a snapshot of children's development at periodic intervals. Assessment gathered over time, both formally and informally, provides a "photo album," rather than a snapshot, of students' progress (Tomlinson & McTighe, 2006). You can use all the information together to adjust and provide appropriate instruction as you go. For instance, based on all your assessment data, you might slow down your instruction, or work one-on-one with a student who isn't "getting it." You can also send home a page that the student worked on in class and ask the family to help the student review the skill.

Multisensory Activities

Before or after children work on an activity page, or on review days (Fridays), try one of these open-ended literacy-building activities, focusing on the skill taught on the page.

✳ **Stretch!** Before students can use their knowledge of sound-spelling relationships to decode words, they must understand that words are made up of sounds (Adams, 1990). Phonemic awareness is the understanding that a word is made up of a series of separate sounds and is the underlying

References

Adams, M. J. (1990). *Beginning to read: Thinking and learning about print.* Cambridge: Massachusetts Institute of Technology Press.

Blevins, W. (1997). *Phonemic awareness activities for early reading success.* New York: Scholastic.

Blevins, W. (2001). *Building fluency: Lessons and strategies for reading success.* New York: Scholastic.

Blevins, W. (2006). *Phonics From A to Z.* New York: Scholastic.

Clay, M. (1993). *Reading recovery: A guidebook for teachers in training.* Portsmouth, NH: Heinemann.

LaPray, M. & Ross, R. (1969). The graded word list: Quick gauge of reading ability. *Journal of Reading* 12 (4).

Samuels, S. J. (1988). Decoding and automaticity: Helping poor readers become automatic at word recognition. *The Reading Teacher*, 41 (8).

Taylor, B. M. & Nosbush, L. (1983). Oral reading for meaning: A technique for improving word identification skills. *The Reading Teacher* 37.

Tomlinson, C. A. & McTighe, J. (2006). *Integrating differentiated instruction and understanding by design.* Alexandria, VA: ASCD

Weaver, Brenda M. (2009). *Assessments & remediation for K–2.* New York: Scholastic.

idea behind phonics instruction. This sound-segmenting exercise helps students break down words into smaller units and sound them out. To begin, select a word and say it slowly, stretching out each sound, such as /c/.../a/.../t/. Have students follow your lead, then repeat, each time shortening the length of each sound until the separate sounds have been blended smoothly together to sound out the word as a whole: "cat."

❋ **Sky Writing** Great for physical learners, sky writing is a way to reinforce letter shapes and spelling patterns by having students trace letters in the air space right in front of them. For instance, when teaching the consonant blend *st*, have students hold up their index finger and "write" *st* in the air in front of them. You can use sky writing for any letter, letter combination, or even for whole words.

❋ **Word Building** Use index cards and markers to create cards with which students can build words and blend sounds. For instance, if you are teaching short *a*, provide cards labeled with *at, b, c, f, h, m, r,* and *s* so students can form *bat, cat,* and so on. When teaching the consonant blend *dr*, you might label cards with *dr, eam, ess, ag, ive,* and so on. Letter cards can be created and used for almost every phonics skill.

❋ **Class Books** Have students make and illustrate books using the target words they learn in the lessons. For instance, when teaching word families, have students illustrate pages with different pictures that belong to a target word family (such as *pack, sack,* and *tack* for the word family *-ack*), label each page with the name of the picture, and then staple the pages together to make a rhyming book. Similarly, have students create a book about a topic such as "Things We Did Yesterday" with pages featuring words that end in *-ed* (*walked, played, colored, cooked,* and so on).

❋ **Buzz!** Tell students that you are going to say some words that belong together and one that does not belong. When they hear the word that does not belong, students make a *buzz* sound. This game works well for almost any phonics goal. For instance:

- Short vowels (*e*): met, sell, men, yes, *meet.*
- Word families (*-ill*): bill, fill, hill, pill, *wig.*
- Consonant digraphs (*ch-*): chip, cherry, cheese, chair, *drip.*
- Early structural analysis (*-ing*): coming, going, running, walking, *watched.*

❋ **Duck, Duck, Goose** You can use this familiar game to reinforce almost any phonics goal. Simply substitute the target phonics skill for "duck," and a word containing that skill for "goose." For instance, the student who takes the role of "It" might walk around the circle of seated students tapping their heads and saying "*Dr, dr, dr, drive!*" The student who is tapped on the word *drive* jumps up and chases "It" around the circle.

Skills-Tracker Chart

Student: _____ Start Date of Intervention: _____

	Skill	Pages	Date	Dictation Words	Assessment Result
Short Vowels (CVC)	**Week 1**				
	a	13–14		cat, mat, bag, bad, nap	/ 5
	a	15–16		man, van, rat, lap, mad	/ 5
	e	17–18		pen, yes, vet, red, pet	/ 5
	e	19–20		bed, net, men, web, leg	/ 5
	Friday Review			cat, bag, man, lap, bed, yes, pen, pet, men, leg	/ 10
	Week 2				
	i	21–22		pig, six, big, hit, kid	/ 5
	i	23–24		lip, bib, pin, rib, zip	/ 5
	o	25–26		box, pot, hop, log, mom	/ 5
	u	27–28		bug, tub, cup, gum, sun	/ 5
	Friday Review			pig, six, hit, lip, rib, pot, hop, bug, tub, gum	/ 10
Long Vowel Digraphs & Silent *e* (CVC*e*)	**Week 3**				
	ai	29–30		snail, train, wait, rain, mail	/ 5
	ay	31–32		tray, hay, clay, jay, way	/ 5
	ea	33–34		pea, clean, weak, meal, peach	/ 5
	ee	35–36		bee, meet, peel, green, sweep	/ 5
	Friday Review			rain, mail, way, tray, meal, clean, team, sweep, peel, green	/ 10
	Week 4				
	oa	37–38		boat, float, coast, road, foam	/ 5
	silent *e* (a__e)	39–40		cape, late, race, snake, paste	/ 5
	silent *e* (i__e)	41–42		pine, five, time, kite, bike	/ 5
	silent *e* (o__e, u__e)	43–44		cute, mule, hole, note, robe	/ 5
	Friday Review			boat, road, cape, race, five, kite, cute, hole, robe, note	/ 10
Variant Vowels & Diphthongs	**Week 5**				
	ar	45–46		jar, arm, bark, card, yarn	/ 5
	aw	47–48		saw, yawn, paw, draw, crawl	/ 5
	oo (*moon*)	49–50		moon, root, food, zoo, smooth	/ 5
	oo (*book*)	51–52		book, foot, woof, good, cook	/ 5
	Friday Review			arm, bark, card, saw, crawl, draw, moon, food, book, good	/ 10
	Week 6				
	oi	53–54		coin, boil, point, noise, join	/ 5
	ou	55–56		house, out, cloud, round, mouth	/ 5
	ow	57–58		clown, cow, down, owl, town	/ 5
	oy	59–60		boy, toy, loyal, enjoy, soy	/ 5
	Friday Review			coin, noise, house, round, out, cow, clown, down, boy, enjoy	/ 10

Skills-Tracker Chart (page 2)

Student: _____ Start Date of Intervention: _____

	Skill	Pages	Date	Dictation Words	Assessment Result
	Week 7				
	br	61–62		bread, brick, brown, brain, brush	/ 5
	cl	63–64		clock, clam, clip, class, clown	/ 5
	cr	65–66		crab, cry, crop, crow, crash	/ 5
	fl	67–68		flag, floss, flower, float, fly	/ 5
	Friday Review			bread, brown, brick, clock, clip, crab, cry, crop, flag, float	/ 10
	Week 8				
Consonant Blends & Digraphs	**gr**	69–70		grapes, great, green, grin, grass	/ 5
	sl	71–72		sled, slim, slug, slow, sleep	/ 5
	st	73–74		star, stop, store, stem, stay	/ 5
	tr	75–76		train, tree, trip, true, trunk	/ 5
	Friday Review			green, grass, grin, slim, slow, star, stem, stay, tree, train	/ 10
	Week 9				
	ch	77–78		cheese, chin, chop, child, chain	/ 5
	sh	79–80		shark, shell, shirt, shoe, sheep	/ 5
	th	81–82		thumb, thin, thorn, thank, third	/ 5
	wh	83–84		wheel, white, why, what, when	/ 5
	Friday Review			cheese, chain, chop, shell, shirt, thin, thank, white, why, when	/ 10
	Week 10				
	-ack	85–86		track, back, pack, crack, snack	/ 5
	-ell	87–88		bell, well, tell, smell, spell	/ 5
	-est	89–90		nest, vest, chest, rest, best	/ 5
	-ick	91–92		kick, sick, brick, quick, wick	/ 5
	Friday Review			back, pack, track, tell, smell, nest, rest, vest, sick, kick	/ 10
Word Families	**Week 11**				
	-ill	93–94		pill, grill, will, hill, chill	/ 5
	-ink	95–96		wink, link, pink, sink, think	/ 5
	-ock	97–98		clock, sock, rock, lock, block	/ 5
	-ump	99–100		hump, jump, grump, lump, pump	/ 5
	Friday Review			hill, will, pink, sink, think, rock, lock, jump, pump, grump	/ 10
	Week 12				
Early Structural Analysis: Prefixes & Suffixes	**re-**	101–102		rebuild, rewrite, replay, reread, reset	/ 5
	un-	103–104		unhappy, unkind, unsure, unzip, unlucky	/ 5
	-ed	105–106		cooked, talked, washed, mixed, jumped	/ 5
	-ing	107–108		walking, drawing, sleeping, flying, drinking	/ 5
	Friday Review			replay, reset, unkind, unzip, unhappy, talked, washed, jumped, drawing, flying	/ 10

Name _____ Date _____

Look at the picture and say its name. Then color the **a** in the word.

Fill in the Blank

Look at each picture. Write **a** to complete the word. Then say each word aloud.

m __ t　　　　**r __ t**　　　　**b __ t**　　　　**h __ t**

Word Path

Help the **cat** get to its **mat**. Color all the boxes with short **a** words. Read them aloud as you go.

rat	rag	box	tip
bed	ran	hug	top
bib	sat	tap	lap

Name _____ Date _____

Read each sentence. Then fill in the blank with the correct word from the box.

Word Box

jam

nap

bag

bad

The opposite of *good* is _____.

My favorite thing to put on bread is _____.

You carry things in a _____.

If you are tired, you can take a _____.

Read along silently as the "Leader" reads this chant the first time. Then read the "Group" part out loud the next time.

Leader: Short *a* is the /a/ sound.

Group: *A, a, a.*

Leader: *Had*! What's the sound in the middle?

Group: *A, a, a*, that's the sound in the middle.

Leader: *Tag*! What's the sound in the middle?

Group: *A, a, a*, that's the sound in the middle.

Leader: *Dad*! What's the sound in the middle?

Group: *A, a, a*, that's the sound in the middle.

Leader: Short *a*, short *a*, what do you say?

Group: *A, a, a!*

Write about a hat you would like to wear. Use the word ***hat***.

_____

_____

RTI: Easy Phonics Interventions © 2011 by Kama Einhorn, Scholastic Teaching Resources

Name _____ Date _____

Look at the picture and say its name. Then color the **a** in the word.

Fill in the Blank

Look at each picture. Write **a** to complete the word.
Then say each word aloud.

p __ n   v __ n   f __ n   c __ n

Word Path

Help the **rat** get to the **cab**. Color all the boxes with short **a** words.
Read them aloud as you go.

bad	mug	bet	met
mad	map	had	mud
hid	cub	tan	cat

Name _____ Date _____

Show What You Know!

Read each sentence. Then fill in the blank with the correct word from the box.

Another word for *angry* is _____.

A baby might sit on your _____.

A dog's tail can _____.

To find your way, use a _____.

Word Box

map

mad

lap

wag

All Together Now

Read along silently as the "Leader" reads this chant the first time. Then read the "Group" part out loud the next time.

Leader: Short *a* is the /a/ sound.

Group: *A, a, a.*

Leader: *Man*! What's the sound in the middle?

Group: *A, a, a,* that's the sound in the middle.

Leader: *Nap*! What's the sound in the middle?

Group: *A, a, a,* that's the sound in the middle.

Leader: *Bag*! What's the sound in the middle?

Group: *A, a, a,* that's the sound in the middle.

Leader: Short *a*, short *a*, what do you say?

Group: *A, a, a!*

Write It!

Write a sentence about a man you know. Use the word **man**.

_____

_____

RTI: Easy Phonics Interventions © 2011 by Kama Einhorn, Scholastic Teaching Resources

Look at the picture and say its name. Then color the **e** in the word.

Fill in the Blank

Look at each picture. Write **e** to complete the word.
Then say each word aloud.

h __ n

t __ n

m __ n

Word Path

The **pet** needs to go to the **vet**. Help her **get** there. Color all
the boxes with short **e** words. Read them aloud as you go.

men	pen	ten	red
mad	sad	mat	jet
put	sit	pat	leg

Name _____ Date _____

Show What You Know!

Read each sentence. Then fill in the blank with the correct word from the box.

Word Box

pet
yes
ten
bed

The opposite of *no* is _____.

You can sleep on a _____.

The number after nine is _____.

An animal that lives with you is a _____.

All Together Now

Read along silently as the "Leader" reads this chant the first time. Then read the "Group" part out loud the next time.

Leader: Short *e* is the /e/ sound.

Group: *E, e, e.*

Leader: *Pen*! What's the sound in the middle?

Group: *E, e, e,* that's the sound in the middle.

Leader: *Bed*! What's the sound in the middle?

Group: *E, e, e,* that's the sound in the middle.

Leader: *Ten*! What's the sound in the middle?

Group: *E, e, e,* that's the sound in the middle.

Leader: Short *e*, short *e*, what do you say?

Group: *E, e, e!*

Write It!

Do you have a pet? Write about it. Use the word **pet**.
If you do not have a pet, would you like to have one? Write why or why not.

_____

_____

Name _____ Date _____

Look at the picture and say its name. Then color the **e** in the word.

Fill in the Blank

Look at each picture. Write **e** to complete the word.
Then say each word aloud.

 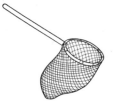 

j __ t   h __ n   n __ t   l __ g

Word Path

The **hen** needs to be **fed**. Help her **get** to her food. Color all
the boxes with short **e** words. Read them aloud as you go.

led	lid	lit	mat
let	met	set	web
pit	sit	put	yet

Name _____ Date _____

Show What You Know!

Read each sentence. Then fill in the blank with the correct word from the box.

A kind of plane is a _____.

The color orange is made from yellow and _____.

The opposite of *dry* is _____.

An animal doctor is called a _____.

Word Box

wet

vet

jet

red

- -

All Together Now

Read along silently as the "Leader" reads this chant the first time. Then read the "Group" part out loud the next time.

Leader: Short *e* is the /e/ sound.

Group: *E, e, e.*

Leader: *Bet*! What's the sound in the middle?

Group: *E, e, e,* that's the sound in the middle.

Leader: *Men*! What's the sound in the middle?

Group: *E, e, e,* that's the sound in the middle.

Leader: *Pet*! What's the sound in the middle?

Group: *E, e, e,* that's the sound in the middle.

Leader: Short *e*, short *e*, what do you say?

Group: *E, e, e!*

- -

Write It!

Write a sentence about something that is red. Use the word **red**.

_____

_____

ame _____ Date _____

Look at the picture and say its name. Then color the **i** in the word.

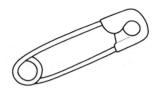 

Fill in the Blank

Look at each picture. Write **i** to complete the word.
Then say each word aloud.

   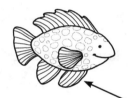

p __ g   s __ x   w __ g   f __ n

Word Path

This **kid** is tired and needs to **sit**. Help **him** get to the chair.
Color all the boxes with short **i** words.
Read them aloud as you go.

bib	dip	fit	bed
hat	rub	hit	tap
mom	tug	rib	tip

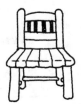

RTI: Easy Phonics Interventions © 2011 by Kama Einhorn, Scholastic Teaching Resources

Name _____ Date _____

Show What You Know!

Read each sentence. Then fill in the blank with the correct word from the box.

The opposite of *small* is _____.

I use a chair when I want to _____.

The opposite of *lose* is _____.

You use a bat to _____ a ball.

Word Box

win

hit

big

sit

All Together Now

Read along silently as the "Leader" reads this chant the first time. Then read the "Group" part out loud the next time.

Leader: Short *i* is the /i/ sound.

Group: I, i, i.

Leader: *Bit*! What's the sound in the middle?

Group: I, i, i, that's the sound in the middle.

Leader: *Did*! What's the sound in the middle?

Group: I, i, i, that's the sound in the middle.

Leader: *Zip*! What's the sound in the middle?

Group: I, i, i, that's the sound in the middle.

Leader: Short *i*, short *i*, what do you say?

Group: I, i, i!

Write It!

Write a sentence about something very large. Use the word **big**.

_____

_____

Name _____ Date _____

Look at the picture and say its name. Then color the *i* in the word.

Fill in the Blank

Look at each picture. Write *i* to complete the word.
Then say each word aloud.

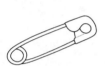  

p __ n   **b __ b**   **l __ p**   **z __ p**

Word Path

This **pig** wants to take a **dip** in the mud. Help **him** get there.
Color all the boxes with short *i* words.
Read them aloud as you go.

pin	bad	hen	rob
bib	top	mug	tag
big	tip	zip	sip

Name _____ Date _____

Show What You Know!

Read each sentence. Then fill in the blank with the correct word from the box.

The number that comes after five is _____.

The end of your finger is called its _____.

You can use a straw to take a little _____.

A bone in your body is a _____.

Word Box

tip

six

sip

rib

All Together Now

Read along silently as the "Leader" reads this chant the first time. Then read the "Group" part out loud the next time.

Leader: Short *i* is the /i/ sound.

Group: I, i, i.

Leader: *Pin*! What's the sound in the middle?

Group: I, i, i, that's the sound in the middle.

Leader: *Lip*! What's the sound in the middle?

Group: I, i, i, that's the sound in the middle.

Leader: *Six*! What's the sound in the middle?

Group: I, i, i, that's the sound in the middle.

Leader: Short *i*, short *i*, what do you say?

Group: I, i, i!

Write It!

Write a sentence about something you did yesterday. Use the word ***did***.

_____

_____

Name _____ Date _____

Look at the picture and say its name. Then color the **o** in the word.

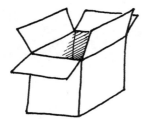 

Look at each picture. Write **o** to complete the word. Then say each word aloud.

f __ x   **l __ g**   **m __ p**   **p __ t**

Help the **fox** find its **mop**. Color all the boxes with short **o** words. Read them aloud as you go.

dot	get	jam	pup
fog	got	job	fed
tag	fun	not	pop

Name _____ Date _____

Show What You Know!

Read each sentence. Then fill in the blank with the correct word from the box.

Another word for *jump* is _____.

The opposite of *cold* is _____.

Another way to say "many" is "a _____."

The opposite of *bottom* is _____.

Word Box

lot

hot

top

hop

All Together Now

Read along silently as the "Leader" reads this chant the first time. Then read the "Group" part out loud the next time.

Leader: Short *o* is the **/o/** sound.

Group: *O, o, o.*

Leader: *Box*! What's the sound in the middle?

Group: *O, o, o,* that's the sound in the middle.

Leader: *Pot*! What's the sound in the middle?

Group: *O, o, o,* that's the sound in the middle.

Leader: *Mom*! What's the sound in the middle?

Group: *O, o, o,* that's the sound in the middle.

Leader: Short *o*, short *o*, what do you say?

Group: *O, o, o!*

Write It!

Write a sentence about something that is hot. Use the word ***hot***.

_____

_____

ame _____ Date _____

Look at the picture and say its name. Then color the **u** in the word.

 **bug**

Fill in the Blank

Look at each picture. Write **u** to complete the word.
Then say each word aloud.

         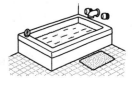

b __ s   **c __ p**   **s __ n**   **t __ b**

 **Word Path**

The **pup** wants to lie in the **sun**. Help him get there.
Color all the boxes with short **u** words.
Read them aloud as you go.

bun	but	bat	dig
mad	dug	not	pet
pad	hug	mud	nut

Name _____ Date _____

Show What You Know!

Read each sentence. Then fill in the blank with the correct word from the box.

Let's get there fast. Let's _____!

You cover the floor with a _____.

A baby bear is called a _____.

I like to chew _____.

Word Box

rug

gum

cub

run

All Together Now

Read along silently as the "Leader" reads this chant the first time. Then read the "Group" part out loud the next time.

Leader: Short *u* is the /u/ sound.

Group: *U, u, u.*

Leader: *Bug*! What's the sound in the middle?

Group: *U, u, u,* that's the sound in the middle.

Leader: *Sun*! What's the sound in the middle?

Group: *U, u, u,* that's the sound in the middle.

Leader: *Cup*! What's the sound in the middle?

Group: *U, u, u,* that's the sound in the middle.

Leader: Short *u*, short *u*, what do you say?

Group: *U, u, u!*

Write It!

Write a sentence about a bug you have seen. Use the word ***bug***.

_____

_____

Name _____ Date _____

Look at the picture and say its name. Then color the **ai** in the word.

snail

Fill in the Blank

Look at each picture. Write **ai** to complete the word.
Then say each word aloud.

br __ __ d **m __ __ l** **n __ __ l** **tr __ __ n**

Word Puzzle

Read the words in the box.
Fit each word into the puzzle going across.
Then write the answer to the riddle.
Use the word spelled out in the shaded boxes.

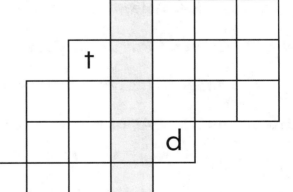

Word Box

drain	tail
praise	trail
laid	

Riddle: How do scientists get to work?

Answer: They take the brain __ __ __ __ __ .

Name _____ Date _____

Show What You Know!

Read each sentence. Then fill in the blank with the correct word from the box.

We have to _____ for the bus.

We took a ride on the bike _____.

I can _____ a picture.

The clouds in the sky might bring _____.

The dog has a _____.

Word Box

tail

paint

trail

wait

rain

All Together Now

Read along silently as the "Leader" reads this chant the first time. Then read the "Group" part out loud the next time.

Leader: Hey, what can you say with *ai*?

Group: *Main, pail, wait.*

Leader: Hey, what can you say with *ai*?

Group: *Rail, train, paint.*

Leader: It's two little letters and one big sound.

Group (loudly):   *Ai, ai, ai!*

Write It!

Write a sentence about a time you saw or rode a train. Use the word **train**.

_____

_____

RTI: Easy Phonics Interventions © 2011 by Kama Einhorn, Scholastic Teaching Resources

Name _____ Date _____

Look at the picture and say its name. Then color the **ay** in the word.

- -

Fill in the Blank

Look at each picture. Write **ay** to complete the word.
Then say each word aloud.

h __ __   **cl** __ __   **s** __ __   **p** __ __

- -

 Word Path

Help the **jay** bird find its **way** to the **hay**. Color all the boxes
with **ay** words. Read them aloud as you go.

bay	lay	ray	spray
boy	dad	bat	tray
red	pat	dot	day

RTI: Easy Phonics Interventions © 2011 by Kama Einhorn, Scholastic Teaching Resources

Name _____ Date _____

Show What You Know!

Read each sentence. Then fill in the blank with the correct word from the box.

Do you want to _____ a game?

Black and white make _____.

It's a sunny _____.

Is this the right _____ to go?

_____ I come in?

Word Box

way
play
gray
may
day

All Together Now

Read along silently as the "Leader" reads this chant the first time. Then read the "Group" part out loud the next time.

Leader: Hey, what can you say with *ay*?

Group: *Hay, pay, clay.*

Leader: Hey, what can you say with *ay*?

Group: *Day, stay, gray.*

Leader: It's two little letters and one big sound.

Group (loudly): *Ay, ay, ay!*

Write It!

Write a sentence about a game you like to play. Use the word *play*.

_____

_____

ame _____ Date _____

Look at the picture and say its name. Then color the **ea** in the word.

Fill in the Blank

Look at each picture. Write **ea** to complete the word.
Then say each word aloud.

p __ __ ch   **m __ __ l**   **s __ __ l**   **b __ __ k**

  Word Path

Help the **seal** find its way to the **beach**. Color all the boxes
with **ea** words. Read them aloud as you go.

sea	tea	teach	say
ten	bed	bead	led
spend	sale	team	speak

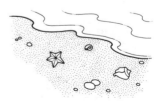

Show What You Know!

Read each sentence. Then fill in the blank with the correct word from the box.

The opposite of *dirty* is _____.

The opposite of *nice* is _____.

The opposite of *fake* is _____.

The opposite of *strong* is _____.

The opposite of *far* is _____.

Word Box

near

weak

clean

mean

real

All Together Now

Read along silently as the "Leader" reads this chant the first time. Then read the "Group" part out loud the next time.

Leader: Hey, what can you say with *ea*?

Group: *Clean*, *meat*, *seal*.

Leader: Hey, what can you say with *ea*?

Group: *Real*, *mean*, *team*.

Leader: It's two little letters and one big sound.

Group (loudly):   *Ea*, *ea*, *ea*!

Write It!

Write a sentence about your favorite meal. It is breakfast, lunch, or dinner? Use the word **meal**.

_____

_____

Look at the picture and say its name. Then color the **ee** in the word.

Look at each picture. Write **ee** to complete the word.
Then say each word aloud.

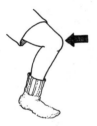   

kn __ __   qu __ __ n   f __ __ t   wh __ __ l

Read the words in the box.
Fit each word into the puzzle going across. Then write the answer to the riddle. Use the word spelled out in the shaded boxes.

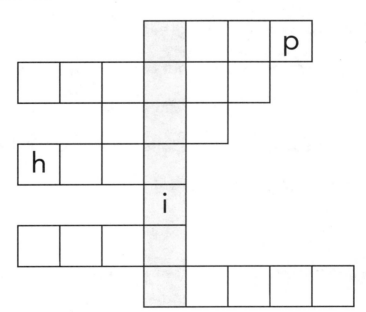

Word Box

street	peep
bee	heel
green	seen

Riddle: What did the banana say to the doctor?

Answer: I'm not __ __ __ __ __ __ __ well.

Name _____ Date _____

Show What You Know!

Read each sentence. Then fill in the blank with the correct word from the box.

Word Box

sweep
peel
meet
green
deep

Use a broom to _____.

Blue and yellow make _____.

The water in the pool is _____.

An orange has a _____.

I'm glad to _____ you!

All Together Now

Read along silently as the "Leader" reads this chant the first time. Then read the "Group" part out loud the next time.

Leader: Hey, what can you say with *ee*?

Group: *Meet, green, three.*

Leader: Hey, what can you say with *ee*?

Group: *Wheel, cheek, sweep.*

Leader: It's two little letters and one big sound.

Group (loudly): *Ee, ee, ee!*

Write It!

Write a sentence about the street you live on. Use the word **street**.

_____

_____

Name _____ Date _____

Look at the picture and say its name. Then color the **oa** in the word.

Fill in the Blank

Look at each picture. Write **oa** to complete the word. Then say each word aloud.

c __ __ t　　　g __ __ t　　　t __ __ d　　　r __ __ d

Word Puzzle

Read the words in the box. Fit each word into the puzzle going across. Then write the answer to the riddle. Use the word spelled out in the shaded boxes.

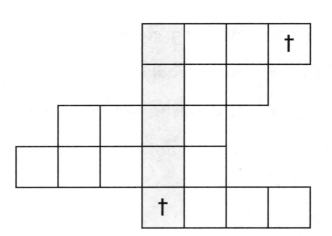

Word Box

oat	roast
toad	coat
foam	

Riddle: Why did the boy ride his bike on the beach?

Answer: He wanted to ___ ___ ___ ___ ___.

Name _____ Date _____

Show What You Know!

Read each sentence. Then fill in the blank with the correct word from the box.

A boat can _____.

I have a sore _____.

I made a _____ in the soccer game.

I like to sit in the bathtub and _____.

The leader of a soccer team is the _____.

Word Box

coach

float

goal

soak

throat

All Together Now

Read along silently as the "Leader" reads this chant the first time. Then read the "Group" part out loud the next time.

Leader: Hey, what can you say with **oa**?

Group: *Coat, goal, foam.*

Leader: Hey, what can you say with **oa**?

Group: *Roast, soak, coach.*

Leader: It's two little letters and one big sound.

Group (loudly): *Oa, oa, oa!*

Write It!

Write a sentence using the words **boat** and **float**.

_____

_____

Name _____ Date _____

One little letter can change the sound of a word. When an **e** comes at the end of a word, the vowel in the word usually says its name. Look at these pictures and say their names. Then color the **e** at the end of the word on the right.

 hat **hat**e

Name the picture on the left. Add an **e** to see how the word changes. Then say the new word aloud.

 cap   changes to   **cap** __

can   changes to   **can** __

Fill in the Blank

Look at each picture. Add an **e** to finish the word. Then say each word aloud.

 cag __   **cak** __   **grap** __   **rak** __

Word Puzzle

Read the words in the box. Fit each word into the puzzle going across. Then write the answer to the riddle. Use the word spelled out in the shaded boxes.

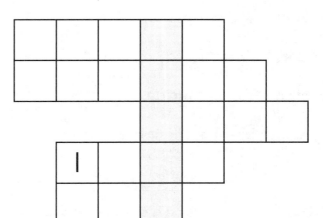

Word Box

age	scrape
paste	same
late	

Riddle: What did the lips say to the tongue?

Answer: "Hey bud, you've got good __ __ __ __ __."

Name _____ Date _____

Show What You Know!

Read each sentence. Then fill in the blank with the correct word from the box.

A long thin animal that hisses is a _____.

You put flowers in a _____.

You can swim in a _____.

You have eyes, a nose, and a mouth on your _____.

The opposite of *early* is _____.

Word Box

snake
lake
face
late
vase

All Together Now

Read along silently as the "Leader" reads this chant the first time. Then read the "Group" part out loud the next time.

Leader: What if I say *past*, but you add an *e*? What happens then?

Group: You get *paste*.

Leader: What if I say *plan*, but you add an *e*? What happens then?

Group: You get *plane*.

Leader: What if I say *mad*, but you add an *e*? What happens then?

Group: You get *made*.

ALL: Silent *e*, silent *e*, keeps on changing words on me!

Write It!

Write a sentence about your favorite place. Use the word *place*.

_____

_____

One little letter can change the sound of a word. When an **e** comes at the end of a word, the vowel in the word usually says its name. Look at these pictures and say their names. Then color the **e** at the end of the word on the right.

 pin **pin**e

Name the picture on the left. Add an **e** to see how each word changes. Then say the new word aloud.

 strip changes to **strip __**

 kit changes to **kit __**

Fill in the Blank

Look at each picture. Add an **e** to finish the word. Then say each word aloud.

 nin __ **vin __** **fiv __** **dim __**

Word Puzzle

Read the words in the box. Fit each word into the puzzle going across. Then write the answer to the riddle. Use the word spelled out in the shaded boxes.

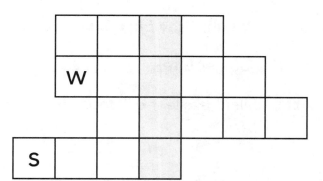

Word Box

| side | bite |
| smile | white |

Riddle: Why did the girl throw the clock out the window?

Answer: She wanted ___ ___ ___ ___ to fly.

Name _____ Date _____

Show What You Know!

Read each sentence. Then fill in the blank with the correct word from the box.

You can _____ into a pool.

I feel _____.

You _____ a car.

Go fly a _____!

You use a pen to _____.

Word Box

kite

drive

write

dive

fine

All Together Now

Read along silently as the "Leader" reads this chant the first time. Then read the "Group" part out loud the next time.

Leader: What if I say *rip*, but you add an *e*? What happens then?

Group: You get *ripe*.

Leader: What if I say *kit*, but you add an *e*? What happens then?

Group: You get *kite*.

Leader: What if I say *bit*, but you add an *e*? What happens then?

Group: You get *bite*.

ALL: Silent *e*, silent *e*, keeps on changing words on me!

Write It!

Write a sentence about riding a bike. Use the word *bike*.

_____

_____

One little letter can change the sound of a word. When an **e** comes at the end of a word, the vowel in the word usually says its name. Look at these pictures and say their names. Then color the **e** at the end of the word on the right.

 cub **cub**e

Name each picture on the left. Add an **e** to see how each word changes. Then say the new word aloud.

 rob   changes to   **rob __**

   cut   changes to   **cut __**

Fill in the Blank

Look at each picture. Add an **e** to finish the word. Then say each word aloud.

 bon __   **mul __**   **glob __**    **smok __**

Word Puzzle

Read the words in the box. Fit each word into the puzzle going across. Then write the answer to the riddle. Use the word spelled out in the shaded boxes.

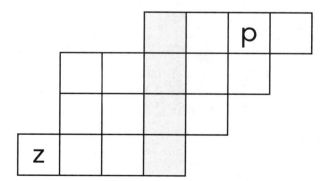

Word Box

mule	zone
hope	smoke

Riddle: What can you put in a wood box to make it lighter?

Answer: A ___ ___ ___ ___.

Show What You Know!

Read each sentence. Then fill in the blank with the correct word from the box.

A block with six square sides is a _____.

An animal in the donkey family is a _____.

You smell with your _____.

You can dig a _____.

You use a pen to write a _____.

Word Box

mule
hole
note
cube
nose

All Together Now

Read along silently as the "Leader" reads this chant the first time. Then read the "Group" part out loud the next time.

Leader: What if I say *glob*, but you add an *e*? What happens then?

Group: You get *globe*.

Leader: What if I say *cut*, but you add an *e*? What happens then?

Group: You get *cute*.

Leader: What if I say *hop*, but you add an *e*? What happens then?

Group: You get *hope*.

ALL: Silent *e*, silent *e*, keeps on changing words on me!

Write It!

Who lives in your home? Write a sentence using the word *home*.

_____

_____

Name _____ Date _____

Look at the picture and say its name. Then color the **ar** in the word.

Look at each picture. Write **ar** to complete the word. Then say each word aloud.

j __ __

b __ __ n

c __ __

__ __ m

? Word Puzzle ?

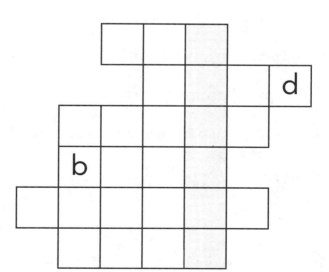

Read the words in the box. Fit each word into the puzzle going across. Then write the answer to the riddle. Use the word spelled out in the shaded boxes.

Word Box

card	dart
sharp	harder
arm	bark

Riddle: Where did the pen go when it first got to town?

Answer: To the __ __ __ __ __ __ .

Name _____ Date _____

Show What You Know!

Read each sentence. Then fill in the blank with the correct word from the box.

Another word for *hurt* is _____.

A sea animal with lots of sharp teeth is a _____.

A student who makes good grades is _____.

We saw a cow, pig, and sheep on the _____.

My grandma knits with a needle and _____.

Word Box

farm

smart

harm

yarn

shark

All Together Now

Read along silently as the "Leader" reads this chant the first time. Then read the "Group" part out loud the next time.

Leader: Hey, what can you say with *ar*?

Group: *Jar, arm, barn.*

Leader: Hey, what can you say with *ar*?

Group: *Farm, yarn, star.*

Leader: It's two little letters and one big sound.

Group (loudly): *Ar, ar, ar!*

Write It!

Write a sentence using the words **star** and **far**.

_____

_____

RTI: Easy Phonics Interventions © 2011 by Kama Einhorn, Scholastic Teaching Resources

Name _____ Date _____

Look at the picture and say its name. Then color the **aw** in the word.

- -

Fill in the Blank   Look at each picture. Write **aw** to complete the word.
Then say each word aloud.

      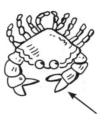   

p __ __   **y __ __ n**   **cl __ __**   **str __ __**

- -

Word Puzzle

Read the words in the box.
Fit each word into the puzzle
going across. Then write the
answer to the riddle. Use
the word spelled out in the
shaded boxes.

Word Box

awful

pawn

strawberry

Riddle: What is a dog's favorite pizza?

Answer: "__ __ __ "-peroni!

Show What You Know!

Read each sentence. Then fill in the blank
with the correct word from the box.

I use crayons to _____ on paper.

Babies _____ on their hands and knees.

A cat's foot is called a _____.

Something that is not cooked is _____.

The grass around a home is called a _____.

Word Box

crawl

paw

draw

lawn

raw

All Together Now

Read along silently as the "Leader" reads this chant the first time.
Then read the "Group" part out loud the next time.

Leader: Hey, what can you say with *aw*?

Group: *Paw, yawn, crawl.*

Leader: Hey, what can you say with *aw*?

Group: *Claw, lawn, draw.*

Leader: It's two little letters and one big sound.

Group (loudly):   *Aw, aw, aw!*

Write It!

Write a sentence about a cat, dog, tiger, or fox. Use the word *paw*.

_____

_____

Name _____ Date _____

Look at the picture and say its name. Then color the **oo** in the word.

Fill in the Blank

Look at each picture. Write **oo** to complete the word.
Then say each word aloud.

ball __ __ n

br __ __ m

g __ __ se

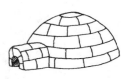

igl __ __

Word Puzzle

Read the words in the box.
Fit each word into the puzzle going
across. Then write the answer to the
riddle. Use the word spelled out in the
shaded boxes.

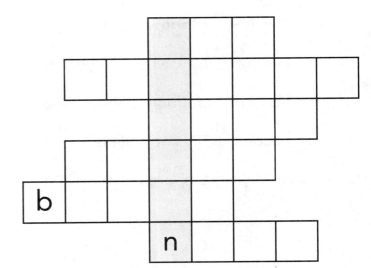

Word Box

broom	moose
boo	shampoo
noon	boot

Riddle: What kind of monkey can fly?

Answer: A hot air __ __ __ __ __ __.

Name _____ Date _____

Show What You Know!

Read each sentence. Then fill in the blank with the correct word from the box.

A cow says _____.

The opposite of *tight* is _____.

The opposite of *rough* is _____.

One part of a plant is its _____.

You can see animals at a _____.

Word Box

smooth

root

zoo

loose

moo

All Together Now

Read along silently as the "Leader" reads this chant the first time. Then read the "Group" part out loud the next time.

Leader: Hey, what can you say with *oo*?

Group: *Moon, zoo, root.*

Leader: Hey, what can you say with *oo*?

Group: *Balloon, broom, goose.*

Leader: It's two little letters and one big sound.

Group (loudly): *Oo, oo, oo!*

Write It!

Write a sentence about your favorite food. Use the word *food*.

_____

_____

Name _____ Date _____

Look at the picture and say its name. Then color the **oo** in the word.

Fill in the Blank

Look at each picture. Write **oo** to complete the word.
Then say each word aloud.

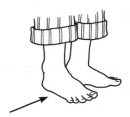   

f __ __ t   h __ __ f   w __ __ d   c __ __ kie

Word Puzzle

Read the words in the box.
Fit each word into the puzzle
going across. Then write the
answer to the riddle. Use the word
spelled out in the shaded boxes.

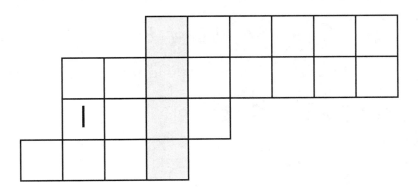

Word Box

hoof   look

wooden   football

Riddle: What does a watchdog sound like?

Answer: Tick, tock, __ __ __ __ !

Show What You Know!

Read each sentence. Then fill in the blank with the correct word from the box.

You put soup in a pot to _____ it.

A dog says, "_____."

The fish took the bait right off the _____.

I _____ in line for a long time.

My sweater is made of _____.

Word Box

woof

hook

wool

stood

cook

All Together Now

Read along silently as the "Leader" reads this chant the first time. Then read the "Group" part out loud the next time.

Leader: Hey, what can you say with **oo**?

Group: *Good, hoof, look.*

Leader: Hey, what can you say with **oo**?

Group: *Wood, book, foot.*

Leader: It's two little letters and one big sound.

Group (loudly):   *Oo, oo, oo!*

Write It!

Write a sentence about a book you like. Use the words **good** and **book**.

_____

_____

RTI: Easy Phonics Interventions © 2011 by Kama Einhorn, Scholastic Teaching Resources

Name _____ Date _____

Look at the picture and say its name. Then color the *oi* in the word.

Fill in the Blank   Look at each picture. Write *oi* to complete the word.
Then say each word aloud.

__ __ l   b __ __ l   p __ __ nt   s __ __ l

Word Puzzle

Read the words in the box.
Fit each word into the puzzle going
across. Then write the answer to the
riddle. Use the word spelled out in
the shaded boxes.

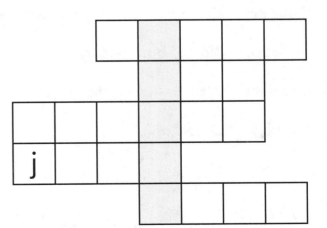

Word Box

toil	oil
choice	spoil
join	

Riddle: What did the pencil say to the pencil sharpener?

Answer: Let's get to the __ __ __ __ __ .

Show What You Know!

Read each sentence. Then fill in the blank with the correct word from the box.

You use your _____ to speak.

When water gets very hot, it will _____.

Do you want to _____ the club?

A drum can make a lot of _____.

Do you want cake or ice cream? It's your _____.

Word Box

join

noise

choice

boil

voice

All Together Now

Read along silently as the "Leader" reads this chant the first time. Then read the "Group" part out loud the next time.

Leader: Hey, what can you say with *oi*?

Group: *Oil, join, choice.*

Leader: Hey, what can you say with *oi*?

Group: *Noise, boil, point.*

Leader: It's two little letters and one big sound.

Group (loudly): *Oi, oi, oi!*

Write It!

Write a sentence about something very loud. Use the word *noise*.

_____

_____

Look at the picture and say its name. Then color the **ou** in the word.

house

Fill in the Blank

Look at each picture. Write **ou** to complete the word. Then say each word aloud.

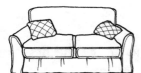

c__ __ ch   cl __ __ d   m __ __ se   m __ __ th

Word Puzzle

Read the words in the box. Fit each word into the puzzle going across. Then write the answer to the riddle. Use the word spelled out in the shaded boxes.

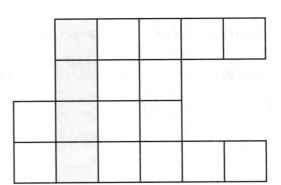

Word Box

ground	ouch
sound	out

Riddle: What do you call a cat that drinks lemonade?

Answer: A __ __ __ __ puss.

Name _____ Date _____

Show What You Know!

Read each sentence. Then fill in the blank with the correct word from the box.

A circle is a _____ shape.

The opposite of *quiet* is _____ .

Another word for *yell* is _____ .

A pig's nose is called a _____ .

The opposite of *lost* is _____ .

Word Box

found

loud

snout

shout

round

All Together Now

Read along silently as the "Leader" reads this chant the first time. Then read the "Group" part out loud the next time.

Leader: Hey, what can you say with *ou*?

Group: *Mouse, couch, cloud.*

Leader: Hey, what can you say with *ou*?

Group: *South, shout, round.*

Leader: It's two little letters and one big sound.

Group (loudly): *Ou, ou, ou!*

Write It!

Write a sentence about a time you felt proud. Use the word **proud**.

_____

_____

Name _____ Date _____

Look at the picture and say its name. Then color the **ow** in the word.

Look at each picture. Write **ow** to complete the word. Then say each word aloud.

c __ __

cr __ __ n

__ __ l

d __ __ n

Word Puzzle

Read the words in the box. Fit each word into the puzzle going across. Then write the answer to the riddle. Use the word spelled out in the shaded boxes.

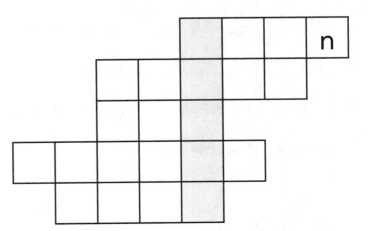

n

Word Box

howl	brown
town	wow
powder	

Riddle: What gets wetter the more it dries?

Answer: A __ __ __ __ __ .

RTI: Easy Phonics Interventions © 2011 by Kama Einhorn, Scholastic Teaching Resources

Name _____ Date _____

Show What You Know!

Read each sentence. Then fill in the blank with the correct word from the box.

A king might wear a _____.

The opposite of *up* is _____.

If you are surprised, you might say "_____!"

Some people live in a small _____.

A large animal that makes milk is a _____.

Word Box

town

wow

cow

down

crown

- -

All Together Now

Read along silently as the "Leader" reads this chant the first time. Then read the "Group" part out loud the next time.

Leader: Hey, what can you say with *ow*?

Group: *Cow, wow, owl.*

Leader: Hey, what can you say with *ow*?

Group: *Crown, town, brown.*

Leader: It's two little letters and one big sound.

Group (loudly): *Ow, ow, ow!*

- -

Write It!

Write a sentence about a time you were surprised. Use the word **wow**.

_____

_____

RTI: Easy Phonics Interventions © 2011 by Kama Einhorn, Scholastic Teaching Resources

Look at the picture and say its name. Then color the **oy** in the word.

Fill in the Blank

Look at each picture. Write **oy** to complete the word.
Then say each word aloud.

 t __ __    **cowb** __ __    **s** __ __

Word Puzzle

Read the words in the box. Fit each word into the puzzle going across. Then write the answer to the riddle. Use the word spelled out in the shaded boxes.

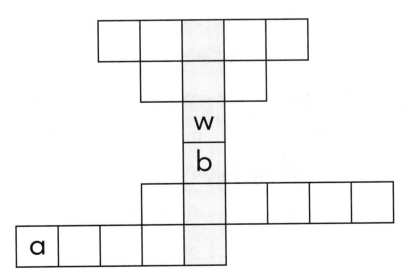

Word Box

voyage	decoy
annoy	toy

Riddle: What has 2 heads, 4 eyes, 6 legs and a tail?

Answer: A __ __ __ __ __ __ riding his horse.

RTI: Easy Phonics Interventions © 2011 by Kama Einhorn, Scholastic Teaching Resources

Show What You Know!

Read each sentence. Then fill in the blank with the correct word from the box.

Another word for *ruin* is _____.

A _____ family lives in the castle.

Playing at the park is something I _____.

My best friend and I are very _____ to each other.

Another word for *trip* is _____.

Word Box

royal

destroy

loyal

enjoy

voyage

All Together Now

Read along silently as the "Leader" reads this chant the first time. Then read the "Group" part out loud the next time.

Leader: Hey, what can you say with *oy*?

Group: *Soy, boy, joy.*

Leader: Hey, what can you say with *oy*?

Group: *Annoy, enjoy, destroy.*

Leader: It's two little letters and one big sound.

Group (loudly): *Oy, oy, oy!*

Write It!

Write a sentence about a time you felt really happy. Use the word *joy*.

_____

_____

Name _____ Date _____

Look at the picture and say its name. Then color the **br** in the word.

br**ead**

Fill in the Blank

Look at each picture. Write **br** to complete the word. Then say each word aloud.

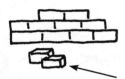         

__ __ **ick**   __ __ **idge**   __ __ **ush**   __ __ **oom**

Word Puzzle

Read the words in the box. Fit each word into the puzzle going across. Then write the answer to the riddle. Use the word spelled out in the shaded boxes.

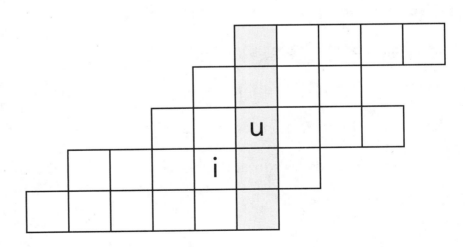

Word Box

brunch	bring
bran	bruise
branch	

Riddle: How do you groom a rabbit?

Answer: With a hare- __ __ __ __ __ .

RTI: Easy Phonics Interventions © 2011 by Kama Einhorn, Scholastic Teaching Resources

Show What You Know!

Read each sentence. Then fill in the blank with the correct word from the box.

Some people wear their hair in a _____.

You think with your _____.

When wind blows, you feel a _____.

The color of soil is _____.

I live with my mother, father, sister, and _____.

Word Box

braid
breeze
brown
brother
brain

All Together Now

Read along silently as the "Leader" reads this chant the first time. Then read the "Group" part out loud the next time.

Leader: *B* and *R* are friends that blend.

Group: *Brain, breeze, brown.*

Leader: *B* and *R* are friends that blend.

Group: *Branch, bring, brush.*

Leader: *B* and *R* are friends that blend.

ALL: Friends 'til the end! Friends 'til the end! *Br, br, br!*

Write It!

Write a sentence about something that is bright. Use the word **bright**.

_____

_____

RTI: Easy Phonics Interventions © 2011 by Kama Einhorn, Scholastic Teaching Resources

Look at the picture and say its name. Then color the **cl** in the word.

Fill in the Blank

Look at each picture. Write **cl** to complete the word. Then say each word aloud.

__ __ **am**

__ __ **oud**

__ __ **ay**

__ __ **own**

Word Puzzle

Read the words in the box. Fit each word into the puzzle going across. Then write the answer to the riddle. Use the word spelled out in the shaded boxes.

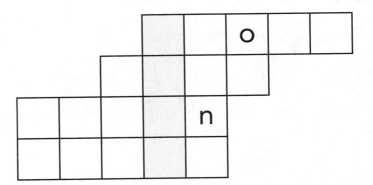

Word Box

| clue | climb |
| cloth | clean |

Riddle: What do you call an underwater music festival?

Answer: A __ __ __ __ jam.

RTI: Easy Phonics Interventions © 2011 by Kama Einhorn, Scholastic Teaching Resources

Name _____ Date _____

Show What You Know!

Read each sentence. Then fill in the blank with the correct word from the box.

Word Box

- climb
- clap
- close
- clip
- closet

To get up a hill, you have to _____.

Hang your clothes in the _____.

You can hold papers together with a paper _____.

You make a sound with your hands when you _____.

Please _____ the door.

All Together Now

Read along silently as the "Leader" reads this chant the first time. Then read the "Group" part out loud the next time.

Leader: *C* and *L* are friends that blend.

Group: *Clap, clip, close.*

Leader: *C* and *L* are friends that blend.

Group: *Climb, class, clown.*

Leader: *C* and *L* are friends that blend.

ALL: Friends 'til the end! Friends 'til the end! *Cl, cl, cl!*

Write It!

Write a sentence about your class. Use the word *class*.

_____

_____

RTI: Easy Phonics Interventions © 2011 by Kama Einhorn, Scholastic Teaching Resources

Name _____ Date _____

Look at the picture and say its name. Then color the **cr** in the word.

Fill in the Blank

Look at each picture. Write **cr** to complete the word.
Then say each word aloud.

__ __ **own**   __ __ **ib**   __ __ **ayon**   __ __ **ack**

Word Puzzle

Read the words in the box.
Fit each word into the puzzle going
across. Then write the answer to
the riddle. Use the word spelled
out in the shaded boxes.

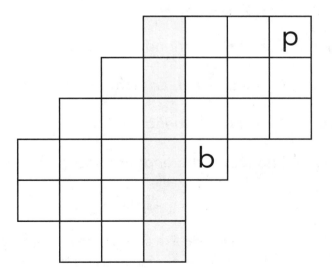

Word Box

cry	crash
crumb	crop
cram	crunch

Riddle: Why did the cookie go to the doctor?

Answer: He was feeling __ __ __ __ __ __.

RTI: Easy Phonics Interventions © 2011 by Kama Einhorn, Scholastic Teaching Resources

65

Name _____ Date _____

Show What You Know!

Read each sentence. Then fill in the blank with the correct word from the box.

Babies often _____ before they walk.

If you are very sad, you might _____.

A bird with shiny black feathers is a _____.

A large group of people in one place is a _____.

A bug that hops is a _____.

Word Box

cry
crowd
crawl
cricket
crow

All Together Now

Read along silently as the "Leader" reads this chant the first time. Then read the "Group" part out loud the next time.

Leader: *C* and *R* are friends that blend.

Group: *Crow, crumb, cry.*

Leader: *C* and *R* are friends that blend.

Group: *Crowd, crawl, crunch.*

Leader: *C* and *R* are friends that blend.

ALL: Friends 'til the end! Friends 'til the end! *Cr, cr, cr!*

Write It!

Do you like sandwiches with or without the crust?
Write a sentence using the word **crust**.

_____

_____

Name _____ Date _____

Look at the picture and say its name. Then color the **fl** in the word.

fl**ag**

Fill in the Blank

Look at each picture. Write **fl** to complete the word. Then say each word aloud.

__ __ y

__ __ oat

__ __ ower

__ __ ute

Word Puzzle

Read the words in the box. Fit each word into the puzzle going across. Then write the answer to the riddle. Use the word spelled out in the shaded boxes.

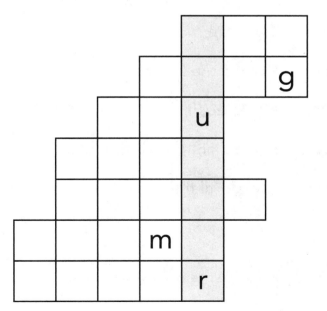

Word Box

flat	flour
flame	flu
fly	flag
flute	

Riddle: What is a butterfly's favorite drink?

Answer: __ __ __ __ __ __ __ milk.

Show What You Know!

Read each sentence. Then fill in the blank with the correct word from the box.

You use _____ to make a cake.

We saw a bright _____ of lightning.

Did you see that large _____ of geese?

My book fell onto the _____ .

I brush my teeth, then I _____ them.

Word Box

flour
floss
flash
floor
flock

All Together Now

Read along silently as the "Leader" reads this chant the first time. Then read the "Group" part out loud the next time.

Leader: *F* and *L* are friends that blend.

Group: *Flag, flip, floss.*

Leader: *F* and *L* are friends that blend.

Group: *Flock, flash, fly.*

Leader: *F* and *L* are friends that blend.

ALL: Friends 'til the end! Friends 'til the end! *Fl, fl, fl!*

Write It!

Write a sentence about something that can fly. Use the word **fly**.

_____

_____

RTI: Easy Phonics Interventions © 2011 by Kama Einhorn, Scholastic Teaching Resources

Name _____   Date _____

Look at the picture and say its name. Then color the **gr** in the word.

Fill in the Blank

Look at each picture. Write **gr** to complete the word.
Then say each word aloud.

__ __ **asshopper**   __ __ **in**   __ __ **ass**   __ __ **ill**

Read the words in the box. Fit each
word into the puzzle going across.
Then write the answer to the riddle.
Use the word spelled out in the
shaded boxes.

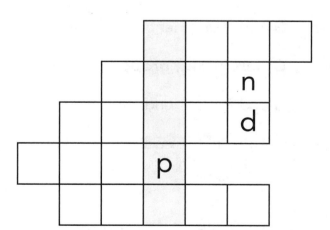

Word Box

grin	green
grand	grip
grow	

Riddle: What did one fruit on the vine say to the other?

Answer: You're __ __ __ __ __ !

Name _____ Date _____

Show What You Know!

Read each sentence. Then fill in the blank with the correct word from the box.

Blue and yellow make _____.

A word that means very good is _____.

If you try to take a dog's bone, it might _____.

Water and sun help a plant to _____.

Another word for *smile* is _____.

Word Box

great
grow
grin
growl
green

All Together Now

Read along silently as the "Leader" reads this chant the first time. Then read the "Group" part out loud the next time.

Leader: *G* and *R* are friends that blend.

Group: *Great, green, gray.*

Leader: *G* and *R* are friends that blend.

Group: *Group, growl, grape.*

Leader: *G* and *R* are friends that blend.

ALL: Friends 'til the end! Friends 'til the end! *Gr, gr, gr!*

Write It!

Write a sentence about something really good that happened to you. Use the word **great**.

_____

_____

ame _____ Date _____

Look at the picture and say its name. Then color the **sl** in the word.

 s**l**ide

---

Fill in the Blank

Look at each picture. Write **sl** to complete the word. Then say each word aloud.

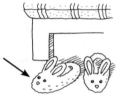

__ __ **ipper**

__ __ **ed**

__ __ **eeve**

__ __ **ug**

Word Puzzle

Read the words in the box. Fit each word into the puzzle going across. Then write the answer to the riddle. Use the word spelled out in the shaded boxes.

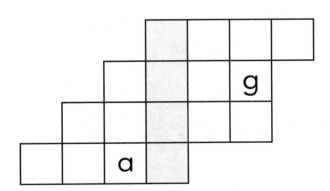

Word Box

| slug | sling |
| slap | slow |

Riddle: What kind of knot should you never step on?

Answer: A ___ ___ ___ ___ knot.

Name _____ Date _____

Show What You Know!

Read each sentence. Then fill in the blank with the correct word from the box.

It's time to close your eyes and _____.

Snow and water mixed together makes _____.

I'd like another _____ of cake.

Another word for *thin* is _____.

The opposite of *fast* is _____.

Word Box

slice
slow
slush
slim
sleep

All Together Now

Read along silently as the "Leader" reads this chant the first time. Then read the "Group" part out loud the next time.

Leader: *S* and *L* are friends that blend.

Group: *Slip*, *slide*, *slush*.

Leader: *S* and *L* are friends that blend.

Group: *Slow*, *slug*, *slime*.

Leader: *S* and *L* are friends that blend.

ALL: Friends 'til the end! Friends 'til the end! *Sl, sl, sl!*

Write It!

Write a sentence about going to sleep. Use the word **sleep**.

_____

_____

ame _____ Date _____

Look at the picture and say its name. Then color the **st** in the word.

Fill in the Blank

Look at each picture. Write **st** to complete the word.
Then say each word aloud.

__ __ **one**

__ __ **op**

__ __ **ove**

__ __ **em**

Word Puzzle

Read the words in the box. Fit each word into the puzzle going across. Then write the answer to the riddle. Use the word spelled out in the shaded boxes.

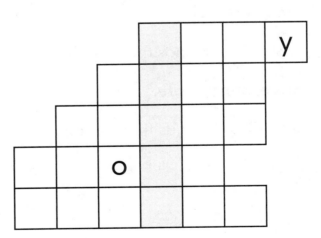

Word Box

stir	stomp
stay	start
staple	

Riddle: What travels around the world but stays in a corner?

Answer: A __ __ __ __ __ .

Name _____ Date _____

Show What You Know!

Read each sentence. Then fill in the blank with the correct word from the box.

You can walk up or down the _____.

The opposite of *go* is _____.

A train stops at a _____.

You buy things in a _____.

My favorite _____ is in this book.

Word Box

stop

stairs

store

story

station

All Together Now

Read along silently as the "Leader" reads this chant the first time. Then read the "Group" part out loud the next time.

Leader: *S* and *T* are friends that blend.

Group: *Stop, start, stay.*

Leader: *S* and *T* are friends that blend.

Group: *Store, story, state.*

Leader: *S* and *T* are friends that blend.

ALL: Friends 'til the end! Friends 'til the end! *St, st, st!*

Write It!

Write a sentence about the state you live in. Use the word **state**.

_____

_____

Look at the picture and say its name. Then color the **tr** in the word.

Fill in the Blank

Look at each picture. Write **tr** to complete the word.
Then say each word aloud.

__ __ ee   __ __ unk   __ __ ay   __ __ umpet

Word Puzzle

Read the words in the box. Fit each word into the puzzle going across. Then write the answer to the riddle. Use the word spelled out in the shaded boxes.

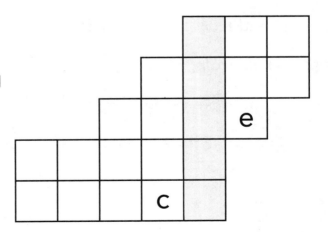

Word Box

train	try
true	trip
track	

Riddle: Where does an elephant pack its clothes?

Answer: In its ___ ___ ___ ___ ___ .

RTI: Easy Phonics Interventions © 2011 by Kama Einhorn, Scholastic Teaching Resources

Name _____ Date _____

Show What You Know!

Read each sentence. Then fill in the blank with the correct word from the box.

The opposite of *false* is _____.

A train travels on a _____.

Yesterday, our class took a field _____.

I like to _____ on planes and trains.

My brother played a _____ on me.

Word Box

travel

trip

true

trick

track

All Together Now

Read along silently as the "Leader" reads this chant the first time. Then read the "Group" part out loud the next time.

Leader: *T* and *R* are friends that blend.

Group: *Tray, true, try.*

Leader: *T* and *R* are friends that blend.

Group: *Trick, train, trunk.*

Leader: *T* and *R* are friends that blend.

ALL: Friends 'til the end! Friends 'til the end! *Tr, tr, tr!*

Write It!

Think about something new that you would like to try. Write a sentence about it. Use the word ***try***.

_____

_____

ame _____ Date _____

Look at the picture and say its name. Then color the **ch** in the word.

Fill in the Blank

Look at each picture. Write **ch** to complete the word.
Then say each word aloud.

__ __ **ain**   __ __ **air**   __ __ **erry**   __ __ **icken**

Word Puzzle

Read the words in the box. Fit each
word into the puzzle going across.
Then write the answer to the riddle.
Use the word spelled out in the
shaded boxes.

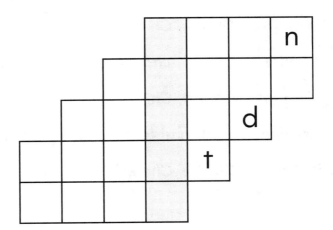

Word Box

chart	child
chin	chase
chop	

Riddle: What is a bird's favorite kind of cookie?

Answer: Chocolate __ __ __ __ __!

Name _____ Date _____

Show What You Know!

Read each sentence. Then fill in the blank with the correct word from the box.

Word Box

chapter

chin

chew

cheap

chalk

You write on the blackboard with _____.

The opposite of *expensive* is _____.

I just read the last _____ in my book.

You use your teeth to _____.

Your _____ is under your mouth.

All Together Now

Read along silently as the "Leader" reads this chant the first time. Then read the "Group" part out loud the next time.

Leader: Put *C* and *H* together for a whole new sound.

Group: *Ch, Ch, Ch.*

Leader: *Chin, chop, chair*—what do you hear?

Group: *Ch, Ch, Ch.*

Leader: *Cherry, chocolate, chicken*—what do you hear?

Group: *Ch, Ch, Ch.*

Leader: Put *C* and *H* together for a whole new sound.

Group (loudly): *Ch, Ch, Cheer!*

Write It!

Write a sentence about a time you felt cheerful. Use the word **cheerful**.

_____

_____

RTI: Easy Phonics Interventions © 2011 by Kama Einhorn, Scholastic Teaching Resources

ame _____ Date _____

Look at the picture and say its name. Then color the **sh** in the word.

sh**ark**

Look at each picture. Write **sh** to complete the word.
Then say each word aloud.

__ __ irt   __ __ ovel   __ __ oe   __ __ eep

Word Puzzle

Read the words in the box. Fit each word
into the puzzle going across. Then write
the answer to the riddle. Use the word
spelled out in the shaded boxes.

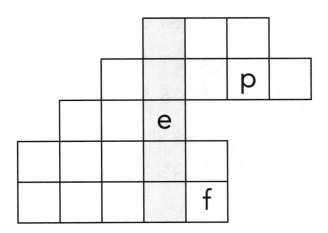

Word Box

shell	shape
shelf	she
shy	

Riddle: What ocean critters never share with others?

Answer: __ __ __ __ __ -fish.

Name _____ Date _____

Show What You Know!

Read each sentence. Then fill in the blank with the correct word from the box.

The opposite of *open* is _____.

The opposite of *tall* is _____.

You go to a store to _____.

You can put books on a _____.

Be careful, the knife is _____.

Word Box

shop
sharp
shelf
short
shut

All Together Now

Read along silently as the "Leader" reads this chant the first time. Then read the "Group" part out loud the next time.

Leader:　Put **S** and **H** together for a whole new sound.

Group:　*Sh, Sh, Sh.*

Leader:　*Shirt, shoe, ship*—what do you hear?

Group:　*Sh, Sh, Sh.*

Leader:　*Short, sharp, shut*—what do you hear?

Group:　*Sh, Sh, Sh.*

Leader:　Put **S** and **H** together for a whole new sound.

Group (loudly):　*Sh, Sh, Sh!*

Write It!

Write a sentence about your favorite shoes. Use the word **shoes**.

_____

_____

RTI: Easy Phonics Interventions © 2011 by Kama Einhorn, Scholastic Teaching Resources

Look at the picture and say its name. Then color the **th** in the word.

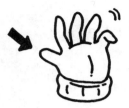 t**h**umb

---

Fill in the Blank   Look at each picture. Write **th** to complete the word. Then say each word aloud.

__ __ ird

__ __ orn

30

__ __ irty

__ __ ermometer

Word Puzzle

Read the words in the box. Fit each word into the puzzle going across. Then write the answer to the riddle. Use the word spelled out in the shaded boxes.

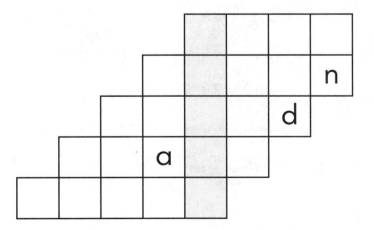

Word Box

thank	thorn
third	thick
thin	

Riddle: Why did the boat skip school?

Answer: It was afraid it would ___ ___ ___ ___ ___ !

Show What You Know!

Read each sentence. Then fill in the blank with the correct word from the box.

I came in _____ place in the race.

Our rose bush has lots of _____.

You use your brain to _____.

The opposite of *thick* is _____.

Your hand has four fingers and a _____.

Word Box

think
thumb
third
thin
thorns

All Together Now

Read along silently as the "Leader" reads this chant the first time. Then read the "Group" part out loud the next time.

Leader: Put *T* and *H* together for a whole new sound.

Group: *Th, Th, Th.*

Leader: *Think, thank, thump*—what do you hear?

Group: *Th, Th, Th.*

Leader: *Thin, thick, thumb*—what do you hear?

Group: *Th, Th, Th.*

Leader: Put *T* and *H* together for a whole new sound.

Group (loudly): *Th, Th, Th!*

Write It!

Write a sentence about something you like to drink. Use the word **thirsty**.

_____

_____

Look at the picture and say its name. Then color the **wh** in the word.

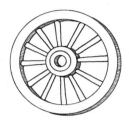 

Fill in the Blank

Look at each picture. Write **wh** to complete the word.
Then say each word aloud.

__ __ **ale**   __ __ **istle**   __ __ **isker**   __ __ **isper**

Word Puzzle

Read the words in the box. Fit each word
into the puzzle going across. Then write
the answer to the riddle. Use the word
spelled out in the shaded boxes.

			p	

Word Box

whopper	whack
what	whip

Riddle: What did the sad horse say to his friends?

Answer: __ __ __ __ is me!

Name _____ Date _____

Show What You Know!

Read each sentence. Then fill in the blank with the correct word from the box.

I want to _____ a secret in your ear.

The opposite of *black* is _____.

The baker just baked a loaf of _____ bread.

A word used to ask a question is _____.

A _____ is a large sea animal.

Word Box

wheat

why

whale

white

whisper

All Together Now

Read along silently as the "Leader" reads this chant the first time. Then read the "Group" part out loud the next time.

Leader: Hey, what can you say with **W** and **H**?

Group: *What*, *when*, *where*.

Leader: Hey, what can you say with **W** and **H**?

Group: *Wheel*, *white*, *why*.

Leader: Put **W** and **H** together and what do you hear?

Group: *Wh*, *wh*, *wh*.

Write It!

Write a sentence about a white whale. Use the words **white** and **whale**.

_____

_____

Look at the picture and say its name. Then color **ack** in the word.

Fill in the Blank

Look at each picture. Write **ack** to complete the word. Then say each word aloud.

st __ __ __   **b** __ __ __   **tr** __ __ __   **qu** __ __ __

Word Puzzle

Read the words in the box. Fit each word into the puzzle going across. Then write the answer to the riddle. Use the word spelled out in the shaded boxes.

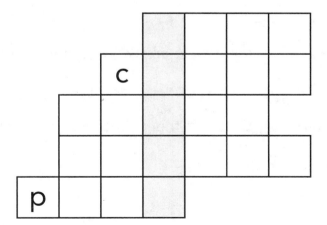

Word Box

pack   racket
tack   snack
crack

Riddle: What is the best advice to give a lost train?

Answer: Try to get back on ___ ___ ___ ___ ___.

Name _____ Date _____

Show What You Know!

Read each sentence. Then fill in the blank with the correct word from the box.

The opposite of *white* is _____.

Another word for *pin* is _____.

A pile of books or papers is called a _____.

Another word for *hit* is _____.

A duck says "_____."

Word Box

stack
tack
black
quack
whack

All Together Now

Read along silently as the "Leader" reads this chant the first time. Then read the "Group" part out loud the next time.

Leader: *A, C, K*. Put them together, and what do they say?

Group: *Ack, ack, ack.*

Leader: *Back, pack, sack*. What sound do they have?

Group: *Ack, ack, ack.*

Leader: *Black, track, crack*. What sound do they have?

Group: *Ack, ack, ack.*

Leader: *A, C, K*. Put them together, and what do they say?

Group: *Ack, ack, ack*!

Write It!

Write a sentence about a duck. Use the word **quack**.

_____

_____

RTI: Easy Phonics Interventions © 2011 by Kama Einhorn, Scholastic Teaching Resources

Name _____ Date _____

Look at the picture and say its name. Then color **ell** in the word.

Fill in the Blank

Look at each picture. Write **ell** to complete the word. Then say each word aloud.

sh __ __ __   **sm** __ __ __   **y** __ __ __   **w** __ __ __

Word Puzzle

Read the words in the box. Fit each word into the puzzle going across. Then write the answer to the riddle. Use the word spelled out in the shaded boxes.

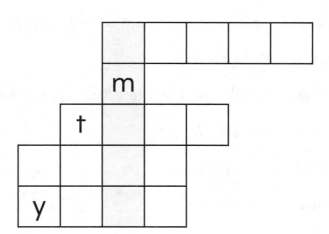

Word Box

| spell | yell |
| tell | well |

Riddle: What did one eye say to the other?

Answer: Between you and me,

something __ __ __ __ __ s!

Name _____ Date _____

Show What You Know!

Read each sentence. Then fill in the blank with the correct word from the box.

Another word for *odor* is _____.

Put prices on the things you want to _____.

I tripped on a rock and _____.

Another word for *shout* is _____.

I found this pretty _____ at the beach.

Word Box

fell

smell

yell

shell

sell

All Together Now

Read along silently as the "Leader" reads this chant the first time. Then read the "Group" part out loud the next time.

Leader: *E, L, L.* Put them together, and what do they say?

Group: *Ell, ell, ell.*

Leader: *Fell, sell, tell.* What sound do they have?

Group: *Ell, ell, ell.*

Leader: *Shell, smell, spell.* What sound do they have?

Group: *Ell, ell, ell.*

Leader: *E, L, L.* Put them together, and what do they say?

Group: *Ell, ell, ell!*

Write It!

Write a sentence about something you do well. Use the word **well**.

_____

_____

Name _____ Date _____

Look at the picture and say its name. Then color **est** in the word.

- -

Fill in the Blank

Look at each picture. Write **est** to complete the word. Then say each word aloud.

   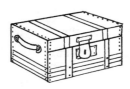   

r __ __ __   v __ __ __   ch __ __ __   w __ __ __

- -

Word Puzzle

Read the words in the box. Fit each word into the puzzle going across. Then write the answer to the riddle. Use the word spelled out in the shaded boxes.

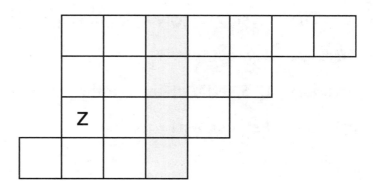

Word Box

| west | guest |
| contest | zest |

Riddle: What did the bird say to the fly?

Answer: You're a pest in my ___ ___ ___ ___ .

Name _____ Date _____

Show What You Know!

Read each sentence. Then fill in the blank with the correct word from the box.

The opposite of *east* is _____.

If you are tired, take a _____.

A sweater without sleeves is called a _____.

I love chocolate ice cream _____ of all.

A visitor in my home is my _____.

Word Box

vest

best

rest

guest

west

All Together Now

Read along silently as the "Leader" reads this chant the first time. Then read the "Group" part out loud the next time.

Leader: *E, S, T*. Put them together, and what do they say?

Group: *Est, est, est*.

Leader: *Best, nest, test*. What sound do they have?

Group: *Est, est, est*.

Leader: *Rest, vest, chest*. What sound do they have?

Group: *Est, est, est*.

Leader: *E, S, T*. Put them together, and what do they say?

Group: *Est, est, est*!

Write It!

Write a sentence about the best thing that has ever happened to you. Use the word **best**.

_____

_____

Name _____ Date _____

Look at the picture and say its name. Then color **ick** in the word.

Fill in the Blank   Look at each picture. Write **ick** to complete the word.
Then say each word aloud.

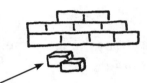      

br __ __ __   k __ __ __   st __ __ __   w __ __ __

? Word Puzzle ?

Read the words in the box. Fit each word
into the puzzle going across. Then write
the answer to the riddle. Use the word
spelled out in the shaded boxes.

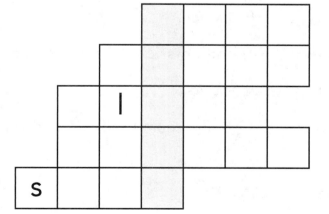

Word Box

sick	brick
tick	tickle
click	

Riddle: What does a fast magician perform?

Answer: A quick ___ ___ ___ ___ ___.

Name _____ Date _____

Show What You Know!

Read each sentence. Then fill in the blank with the correct word from the box.

The opposite of *thin* is _____.

A strong house might be made of _____.

A clock goes _____-tock.

The opposite of *healthy* is _____.

Another word for *fast* is _____.

Word Box

sick

quick

thick

tick

brick

All Together Now

Read along silently as the "Leader" reads this chant the first time. Then read the "Group" part out loud the next time.

Leader: *I, C, K*. Put them together, and what do they say?

 Group: *Ick, ick, ick.*

Leader: *Kick, lick, pick*. What sound do they have?

 Group: *Ick, ick, ick.*

Leader: *Brick, click, stick*. What sound do they have?

 Group: *Ick, ick, ick.*

Leader: *I, C, K*. Put them together, and what do they say?

 Group: *Ick, ick, ick!*

Write It!

Write a sentence about something you can do very fast. Use the word *quick*.

_____

_____

Name _____ Date _____

Look at the picture and say its name. Then color **ill** in the word.

Fill in the Blank   Look at each picture. Write **ill** to complete the word.
Then say each word aloud.

gr __ __ __   **p** __ __ __   **dr** __ __ __   **sp** __ __ __

Word Puzzle

Read the words in the box. Fit each
word into the puzzle going across.
Then write the answer to the riddle.
Use the word spelled out in the
shaded boxes.

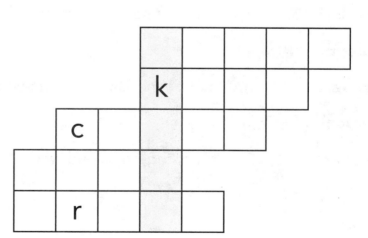

Word Box

frill	kill
spill	chill
bill	

Riddle: What makes an open-grill chef so good?

Answer: His grill ___ ___ ___ ___ ___.

Name _____ Date _____

Show What You Know!

Read each sentence. Then fill in the blank with the correct word from the box.

Another word for *sick* is _____.

Jack and Jill went up the _____.

Another word for *cold* is _____.

We like to cook hot dogs on the _____.

I wrote a check to pay the water _____.

Word Box

chill
bill
hill
grill
ill

All Together Now

Read along silently as the "Leader" reads this chant the first time. Then read the "Group" part out loud the next time.

Leader: *I, L, L.* Put them together, and what do they say?

Group: *Ill, ill, ill.*

Leader: *Fill, hill, will.* What sound do they have?

Group: *Ill, ill, ill.*

Leader: *Chill, grill, spill.* What sound do they have?

Group: *Ill, ill, ill.*

Leader: *I, L, L.* Put them together, and what do they say?

Group: *Ill, ill, ill!*

Write It!

Write a sentence about something you will do today. Use the word **will**.

_____

_____

Look at the picture and say its name. Then color **ink** in the word.

Fill in the Blank

Look at each picture. Write **ink** to complete the word. Then say each word aloud.

w __ __ __

l__ __ __

dr __ __ __

st __ __ __

Word Puzzle

Read the words in the box. Fit each word into the puzzle going across. Then write the answer to the riddle. Use the word spelled out in the shaded boxes.

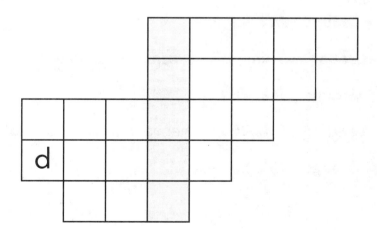

Word Box

shrink	link
brink	ink
drink	

Riddle: What can you never watch yourself do in a mirror?

Answer: __ __ __ __ __.

Name _____ Date _____

Show What You Know!

Read each sentence. Then fill in the blank with the correct word from the box.

You wash dishes in a _____.

When I do math, I really have to _____.

Mix red and white together to make _____.

You can go ice-skating in a _____.

When the weather is cold, I like a hot _____.

Word Box

drink

rink

sink

pink

think

All Together Now

Read along silently as the "Leader" reads this chant the first time. Then read the "Group" part out loud the next time.

Leader: *I, N, K*. Put them together, and what do they say?

Group: *Ink, ink, ink.*

Leader: *Pink, sink, wink*. What sound do they have?

Group: *Ink, ink, ink.*

Leader: *Think, blink, drink*. What sound do they have?

Group: *Ink, ink, ink.*

Leader: *I, N, K*. Put them together, and what do they say?

Group: *Ink, ink, ink!*

Write It!

Write a sentence about something that is pink. Use the word **pink**.

_____

_____

RTI: Easy Phonics Interventions © 2011 by Kama Einhorn, Scholastic Teaching Resources

Name _____ Date _____

Look at the picture and say its name. Then color **ock** in the word.

Fill in the Blank

Look at each picture. Write **ock** to complete the word. Then say each word aloud.

s __ __ __   bl __ __ __   l __ __ __   r __ __ __

Word Puzzle

Read the words in the box. Fit each word into the puzzle going across. Then write the answer to the riddle. Use the word spelled out in the shaded boxes.

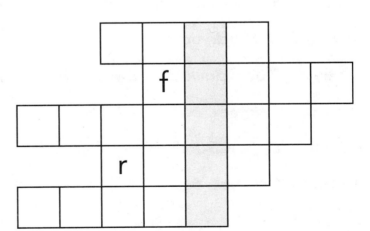

Word Box

knock	flock
dock	rock
peacock	

Riddle: What has two hands but can't clap?

Answer: A __ __ __ __ __ .

Name _____ Date _____

Show What You Know!

Read each sentence. Then fill in the blank with the correct word from the box.

When I leave, I always _____ the door.

You can leave a boat at a _____.

I fell off my bike when I ran over a _____.

Some birds fly in a _____.

Another word for *surprise* is _____.

Word Box

shock

dock

flock

lock

rock

All Together Now

Read along silently as the "Leader" reads this chant the first time. Then read the "Group" part out loud the next time.

Leader: *O, C, K.* Put them together, and what do they say?

 Group: *Ock, ock, ock.*

Leader: *Rock, sock, lock.* What sound do they have?

 Group: *Ock, ock, ock.*

Leader: *Block, clock, shock.* What sound do they have?

 Group: *Ock, ock, ock.*

Leader: *O, C, K.* Put them together, and what do they say?

 Group: *Ock, ock, ock!*

Write It!

Write a sentence about a magic clock. Use the word **clock**.

_____

_____

RTI: Easy Phonics Interventions © 2011 by Kama Einhorn, Scholastic Teaching Resources

Name _____ Date _____

Look at the picture and say its name. Then color **ump** in the word.

hump

Fill in the Blank

Look at each picture. Write **ump** to complete the word. Then say each word aloud.

j_ _ _

st _ _ _

l_ _ _

gr _ _ _

Word Puzzle

Read the words in the box. Fit each word into the puzzle going across. Then write the answer to the riddle. Use the word spelled out in the shaded boxes.

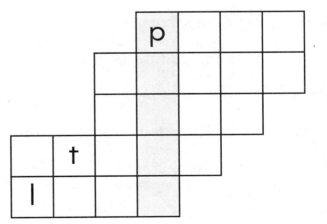

Word Box

stump   clump
pump   jump
lump

Riddle: What do you call a fat plum?

Answer: __ __ __ __ __ .

Name _____ Date _____

Show What You Know!

Read each sentence. Then fill in the blank with the correct word from the box.

I try to stir out every _____ in my cake batter.

To fix a flat tire, you need a _____.

The book I dropped landed with a _____.

A camel has a _____.

When I'm in a bad mood, I can be a _____.

All Together Now

Read along silently as the "Leader" reads this chant the first time. Then read the "Group" part out loud the next time.

Leader: U, M, P. Put them together, and what do they say?

Group: Ump, ump, ump.

Leader: Bump, jump, lump. What sound do they have?

Group: Ump, ump, ump.

Leader: Grump, stump, thump. What sound do they have?

Group: Ump, ump, ump.

Leader: U, M, P. Put them together, and what do they say?

Group: Ump, ump, ump!

Write It!

Write a sentence about a time when you felt like a grump. Use the word **grump**.

_____

_____

Name _____ Date _____

When you see **re-** in front of an action word, take away that part of the word. If a complete word remains, then the **re-** usually means **again**—the action is or will be repeated. Look at this picture and read the action word. Then color the **re** in the word.

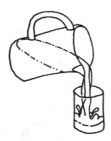 

refill

| Fill in the Blank | Look at each picture and its word. Add **re-** to show that the action will be repeated. Then say each word aloud. |

	Action	Repeat Action
	read	__ __ read
	write	__ __ write
	build	__ __ build
	play	__ __ play
	set	__ __ set

RTI: Easy Phonics Interventions © 2011 by Kama Einhorn, Scholastic Teaching Resources

Show What You Know!

Read each sentence. Then fill in the blank with the correct word from the box.

Word Box

rewash
rewrite
restack
resweep
remake

If you sweep the floor again, you _____ it.

When you wash a dish again, you _____ it.

If you make your bed again, you _____ it.

When you stack your books again, you _____ them.

If you write the same sentence again, you _____ it.

All Together Now

Read along silently as the "Leader" reads this chant the first time. Then read the "Group" part out loud the next time.

Leader: When *re-*, *re-*, *re-* is in front of a word, it means…

Group: *Again, again, again.*

Leader: *Reread*! What does it mean?

Group: *Read again.*

Leader: *Rewrite*! What does it mean?

Group: *Write again.*

Leader: *Redo*! What does it mean?

Group: *Do again.*

Leader: When *re-*, *re-*, *re-* is in front of a word, it means…

Group: *Again, again, again.*

Write It!

Write a sentence about a book you would like to read again. Use the word **reread**.

_____

_____

When you see **un-** in front of a word, take away that part of the word. If a complete word remains, then the **un-** usually means **not**—it changes the word's meaning to just the opposite. Look at this picture and read the word. Then color the **un** in the word.

The girl is unhappy.

Fill in the Blank Look at each picture and its word. Add **un-** to show the opposite meaning of that word. Then say each word aloud.

	Word	Opposite
	zip	__ __ zip
	well	__ __ well
	afraid	__ __ afraid
	even	__ __ even
	dress	__ __ dress

Show What You Know!

Read each sentence. Then fill in the blank with the correct word from the box.

A word that means *not nice* is _____.

When you can't do something, you are _____ to do it.

If you can't make up your mind, you are _____.

Another word for *sick* is _____.

When people lie, they say something _____.

Word Box

unsure

unkind

untrue

unwell

unable

All Together Now

Read along silently as the "Leader" reads this chant the first time. Then read the "Group" part out loud the next time.

Leader: When *un-, un-, un-* is in front of a word, it means...

Group: *Not, not, not.*

Leader: *Unlucky!* What does it mean?

Group: *Not lucky.*

Leader: *Untrue!* What does it mean?

Group: *Not true.*

Leader: *Unsure!* What does it mean?

Group: *Not sure.*

Leader: When *un-, un-, un-* is in front of a word, it means...

Group: *Not, not, not.*

Write It!

Write a sentence about a very strange thing you have seen or imagined. Use the word **unusual**.

_____

_____

RTI: Easy Phonics Interventions © 2011 by Kama Einhorn, Scholastic Teaching Resources

When you see **-ed** at the end of an action word, that action has already happened. Look at this picture and read the action word. Then color the **ed** in the word.

The boy cooked.

Fill in the Blank

Look at each picture and action word. Add **-ed** to show the action has already happened—it is a **past action**. Then say each word aloud.

	Action	Past Action
	walk	**walk __ __**
	pick	**pick __ __**
	reach	**reach __ __**
	paint	**paint __ __**
	wash	**wash __ __**

Show What You Know!

Read each sentence. Then fill in the blank with the correct word from the box.

Imagine you made a pie yesterday. How did you make it?

First, I _____ the berries.

Next, I _____ butter and flour for the dough.

Then, I _____ the dough into a pan to make the crust.

After that, I _____ the crust with berries.

Finally, I _____ the pie.

Word Box

cooked
mixed
washed
filled
pressed

All Together Now

Read along silently as the "Leader" reads this chant the first time. Then read the "Group" part out loud the next time.

Leader: Add -ed to a verb to show it happened in the past.

Group: It already happened. It happened in the past.

Leader: Today, we *walk*.

Group: Yesterday, we *walked*.

Leader: Today, we *talk*.

Group: Yesterday, we *talked*.

Leader: Add -ed to a verb to show it happened in the past.

Group: It already happened. It happened in the past.

Write It!

Write a sentence about something you did yesterday. Use a word that ends in -ed.

_____

_____

Name _____ Date _____

When you see **-ing** at the end of an action word, that action is happening right now.
Look at this picture and read the action word. Then color the **ing** in the word.

The boy is walking.

Fill in the Blank

Look at each picture and action word. Add **-ing** to show that
the action is happening right now—it is a **present action**.
Then say each word aloud.

	Action	Present Action
	draw	**draw** __ __ __
	read	**read** __ __ __
	drink	**drink** __ __ __
	sleep	**sleep** __ __ __
	jump	**jump** __ __ __

Name _____ Date _____

Show What You Know!

Read each sentence. Then fill in the blank with the correct word from the box.

Imagine you are spending the night in the forest. What is happening right now?

The owls are _____.

The wolves are _____.

The crickets are _____.

The wind is _____.

The trees are _____.

Word Box

chirping
flying
blowing
howling
swaying

All Together Now

Read along silently as the "Leader" reads this chant the first time. Then read the "Group" part out loud the next time.

Leader: -Ing, -ing, -ing. What is happening now?

Group: -Ing, -ing, -ing means something is happening now.

Leader: It's time to read.

Group: We're *reading*!

Leader: It's time to eat.

Group: We're *eating*!

Leader: It's time to walk.

Group: We're *walking*!

Leader: You're *reading*. You're *eating*. You're *walking*.

Group: -Ing, -ing, -ing means something is happening now.

Write It!

Write a sentence about something that is happening right now. Use a word that ends in *-ing*.

_____

_____

Answers

page 13
Fill in the Blank
mat, rat, bat, hat

Word Path

rat	rag	box	tip
bed	ran	hug	top
bib	sat	tap	lap

page 14
Show What You Know!
bad, jam, bag, nap

Write It!: Answers will vary.

page 15
Fill in the Blank
pan, van, fan, can

Word Path

bad	mug	bet	met
mad	map	had	mud
hid	cub	tan	cat

page 16
Show What You Know!
mad, lap, wag, map

Write It! Answers will vary.

page 17
Fill in the Blank: hen, ten, men

Word Path

men	pen	ten	red
mad	sad	mat	jet
put	sit	pat	leg

page 18
Show What You Know!
yes, bed, ten, pet

Write It! Answers will vary.

page 19
Fill in the Blank
jet, hen, net, leg

Word Path

led	lid	lit	mat
let	met	set	web
pit	sit	put	yet

page 20
Show What You Know!
jet, red, wet, vet

Write It!: Answers will vary.

page 21
Fill in the Blank
pig, six, wig, fin

Word Path

bib	dip	fit	bed
hat	rub	hit	tap
mom	tug	rib	tip

page 22
Show What You Know!
big, sit, win, hit

Write It!: Answers will vary.

page 23
Fill in the Blank
pin, bib, lip, zip

Word Path

pin	bad	hen	rob
bib	top	mug	tag
big	tip	zip	sip

page 24
Show What You Know!
six, tip, sip, rib

Write It!: Answers will vary.

page 25
Fill in the Blank
fox, log, mop, pot

Word Path

dot	get	jam	pup
fog	got	job	fed
tag	fun	not	pop

page 26
Show What You Know!
hop, hot, lot, top

Write It!: Answers will vary.

page 27
Fill in the Blank
bus, cup, sun, tub

Word Path

bun	but	bat	dig
mad	dug	not	pet
pad	hug	mud	nut

page 28
Show What You Know!
run, rug, cub, gum

Write It!: Answers will vary.

page 29
Fill in the Blank
braid, mail, nail, train

Word Puzzle

		t	a	i	l	
	t	r	a	i	l	
	p	r	a	i	s	e
		l	a	i	d	
d	r	a	i	n		

Answer: They take the brain train.

page 30
Show What You Know!
wait, trail, paint, rain, tail

Write It!: Answers will vary.

page 31
Fill in the Blank
hay, clay, say, pay

Word Path

bay	lay	ray	spray
boy	dad	bat	tray
red	pat	dot	day

page 32
Show What You Know!
play, gray, day, way, May

Write It!: Answers will vary.

page 33
Fill in the Blank
peach, meal, seal, beak

Word Path

sea	tea	teach	say
ten	bed	bead	led
spend	sale	team	speak

page 34
Show What You Know!
clean, mean, real, weak, near

Write It!: Answers will vary.

page 35
Fill in the Blank
knee, queen, feet, wheel

Word Puzzle

				p	e	e	p
s	t	r	e	e	t		
				b	e	e	
h	e	e	l				
			i				
s	e	e	n				
			g	r	e	e	n

Answer: I'm not peeling well.

page 36
Show What You Know!
sweep, green, deep, peel, meet

Write It!: Answers will vary.

page 37
Fill in the Blank
coat, goat, toad, road

Word Puzzle

		c	o	a	t
		o	a	t	
	f	o	a	m	
r	o	a	s	t	
		t	o	a	d

Answer: He wanted to coast.

page 38
Show What You Know!
float, throat, goal, soak, coach

Write It!: Answers will vary.

page 39

Fill in the Blank
cage, cake, grape, rake

Word Puzzle

p	a	s	t	e	
s	c	r	a	p	e
		s	a	m	e
	l	a	t	e	
	a	g	e		

Answer: "Hey bud, you've got good taste."

page 40

Show What You Know!
snake, vase, lake, face, late

Write It!: Answers will vary.

page 41

Fill in the Blank
nine, vine, five, dime

Word Puzzle

	b	i	t	e	
w	h	i	t	e	
		s	m	i	l	e
s	i	d	e		

Answer: She wanted time to fly.

page 42

Show What You Know!
dive, fine, drive, kite, write

Write It!: Answers will vary.

page 43

Fill in the Blank
bone, mule, globe, smoke

Word Puzzle

		h	o	p	e
	s	m	o	k	e
	m	u	l	e	
z	o	n	e		

Answer: A hole.

page 44

Show What You Know!
cube, mule, nose, hole, note

Write It!: Answers will vary.

page 45

Fill in the Blank
jar, barn, car, arm

Word Puzzle

	a	r	m		
		c	a	r	d
s	h	a	r	p	
b	a	r	k		
h	a	r	d	e	r
d	a	r	t		

Answer: To the market.

page 46

Show What You Know!
harm, shark, smart, farm, yarn

Write It!: Answers will vary.

page 47

Fill in the Blank
paw, yawn, claw, straw

Word Puzzle

		p	a	w	n		
s	t	r	a	w	b	e	r	r	y
		a	w	f	u	l	

Answer: "Paw"-peroni!

page 48

Show What You Know!
draw, crawl, paw, raw, lawn

Write It!: Answers will vary.

page 49

Fill in the Blank
balloon, broom, goose, igloo

Word Puzzle

		b	o	o	
s	h	a	m	p	o	o
		b	o	o	t
	m	o	o	s	e
b	r	o	o	m	
		n	o	o	n

Answer: A hot-air baboon.

page 50

Show What You Know!
moo, loose, smooth, root, zoo

Write It!: Answers will vary.

page 51

Fill in the Blank
foot, hoof, wood, cookie

Word Puzzle

		w	o	o	d	e	n
f	o	o	t	b	a	l	l
		l	o	o	k	
h	o	o	f		

Answer: Tick, tock, woof!

page 52

Show What You Know!
cook, woof, hook, stood, wool

Write It!: Answers will vary.

page 53

Fill in the Blank
oil, boil, point, soil

Word Puzzle

	s	p	o	i	l	
		o	i	l	
c	h	o	i	c	e
j	o	i	n		
	t	o	i	l	

Answer: Let's get to the point.

page 54

Show What You Know!
voice, boil, join, noise, choice

Write It!: Answers will vary.

page 55

Fill in the Blank
couch, cloud, mouse, mouth

Word Puzzle

	s	o	u	n	d	
	o	u	t		
o	u	c	h		
g	r	o	u	n	d

Answer: A sour puss.

page 56

Show What You Know!
round, loud, shout, snout, fo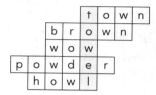

Write It!: Answers will var

page 57

Fill in the Blank
cow, crown, owl, down

Word Puzzle

		t	o	w	n
b	r	o	w	n	
	w	o	w		
p	o	w	d	e	r
h	o	w	l		

Answer: A towel.

page 58

Show What You Know!
crown, down, Wow, town, c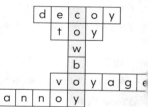

Write It!: Answers will var

page 59

Fill in the Blank
toy, cowboy, soy

Word Puzzle

	d	e	c	o	y	
		t	o	y	
		w			
		b			
	v	o	y	a	g	e
a	n	n	o	y	

Answer: A cowboy riding his horse.

page 60

Show What You Know!
destroy, royal, enjoy, loyal, voyage

Write It!: Answers will vary.

page 61

Fill in the Blank
brick, bridge, brush, broom

Word Puzzle

```
    b r i n g
  b r a n
b r u n c h
b r u i s e
b r a n c h
```

Answer: With a hare–brush.

page 62

Show What You Know!
braid, brain, breeze, brown, brother

Write It!: Answers will vary.

page 63

Fill in the Blank
clam, cloud, clay, clown

Word Puzzle

```
    c l o t h
  c l u e
c l e a n
c l i m b
```

Answer: A clam jam.

page 64

Show What You Know!
climb, closet, clip, clap, close

Write It!: Answers will vary.

page 65

Fill in the Blank
crown, crib, crayon, crack

Word Puzzle

```
    c r o p
  c r a s h
c r u n c h
c r u m b
c r a m
  c r y
```

Answer: He was feeling crummy.

page 66

Show What You Know!
crawl, cry, crow, crowd, cricket

Write It!
Answers will vary.

page 67

Fill in the Blank
fly, float, flower, flute

Word Puzzle

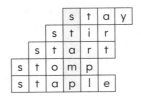

```
    f l y
    f l a g
    f l u
  f l a t
  f l u t e
f l a m e
f l o u r
```

Answer: Flutter-milk.

page 68

Show What You Know!
flour, flash, flock, floor, floss

Write It!: Answers will vary.

page 69

Fill in the Blank
grasshopper, grin, grass, grill

Word Puzzle

```
    g r o w
  g r i n
g r a n d
g r i p
g r e e n
```

Answer: You're grape!

page 70

Show What You Know!
green, great, growl, grow, grin

Write It!: Answers will vary.

page 71

Fill in the Blank
slipper, sled, sleeve, slug

Word Puzzle

```
    s l o w
  s l u g
  s l i n g
s l a p
```

Answer: A slip knot.

page 72

Show What You Know!
sleep, slush, slice, slim, slow

Write It!: Answers will vary.

page 73

Fill in the Blank
stone, stop, stove, stem

Word Puzzle

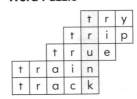

```
    s t a y
  s t i r
s t a r t
s t o m p
s t a p l e
```

Answer: A stamp.

page 74

Show What You Know!
stairs, stop, station, store, story

Write It!: Answers will vary.

page 75

Fill in the Blank
tree, trunk, tray, trumpet

Word Puzzle

```
    t r y
    t r i p
  t r u e
t r a i n
t r a c k
```

Answer: In its trunk.

page 76

Show What You Know!
true, track, trip, travel, trick

Write It!: Answers will vary.

page 77

Fill in the Blank
chain, chair, cherry, chicken

Word Puzzle

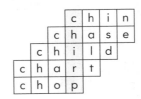

```
    c h i n
  c h a s e
c h i l d
c h a r t
c h o p
```

Answer: Chocolate chirp!

page 78

Show What You Know!
chalk, cheap, chapter, chew, chin

Write It!: Answers will vary.

page 79

Fill in the Blank
shirt, shovel, shoe, sheep

Word Puzzle

```
    s h y
  s h a p e
  s h e
s h e l l
s h e l f
```

Answer: Shell-fish.

page 80

Show What You Know!
shut, short, shop, shelf, sharp

Write It!: Answers will vary.

page 81

Fill in the Blank
third, thorn, thirty, thermometer

Word Puzzle

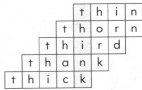

```
      t h i n
    t h o r n
  t h i r d
t h a n k
t h i c k
```

Answer: It was afraid it would think!

page 82

Show What You Know!
third, thorns, think, thin, thumb

Write It!: Answers will vary.

page 83

Fill in the Blank
whale, whistle, whisker, whisper

Word Puzzle

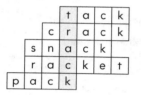

	w	h	a	t		
	w	h	i	p		
w	h	o	p	p	e	r
w	h	a	c	k		

Answer: Whoa is me!

page 84

Show What You Know!
whisper, white, wheat, why, whale

Write It!: Answers will vary.

page 85

Fill in the Blank
stack, back, track, quack

Word Puzzle

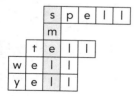

		t	a	c	k	
	c	r	a	c	k	
s	n	a	c	k		
r	a	c	k	e	t	
p	a	c	k			

Answer: Try to get back on track.

page 86

Show What You Know!
black, tack, stack, whack, quack

Write It!: Answers will vary.

page 87

Fill in the Blank
shell, smell, yell, well

Word Puzzle

	s	p	e	l	l
	m				
	t	e	l	l	
w	e	l	l		
y	e	l	l		

Answer: Between you and me, something smells!

page 88

Show What You Know!
smell, sell, fell, yell, shell

Write It!: Answers will vary.

page 89

Fill in the Blank
rest, vest, chest, west

Word Puzzle

c	o	n	t	e	s	t
g	u	e	s	t		
z	e	s	t			
w	e	s	t			

Answer: You're a pest in my nest.

page 90

Show What You Know!
west, rest, vest, best, guest

Write It!: Answers will vary.

page 91

Fill in the Blank
brick, kick, stick, wick

Word Puzzle

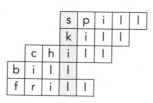

		t	i	c	k	
	b	r	i	c	k	
c	l	i	c	k		
t	i	c	k	l	e	
s	i	c	k			

Answer: A quick trick.

page 92

Show What You Know!
thick, brick, tick, sick, quick

Write It!: Answers will vary.

page 93

Fill in the Blank
grill, pill, drill, spill

Word Puzzle

	s	p	i	l	l
	k	i	l	l	
c	h	i	l	l	
b	i	l	l		
f	r	i	l	l	

Answer: His grill skill.

page 94

Show What You Know!
ill, hill, chill, grill, bill

Write It!: Answers will vary.

page 95

Fill in the Blank
wink, link, drink, stink

Word Puzzle

		b	r	i	n	k
		l	i	n	k	
s	h	r	i	n	k	
d	r	i	n	k		
	i	n	k			

Answer: Blink.

page 96

Show What You Know!
sink, think, pink, rink, drink

Write It!: Answers will vary.

page 97

Fill in the Blank
sock, block, lock, rock

Word Puzzle

	d	o	c	k		
		f	l	o	c	k
p	e	a	c	o	c	k
		r	o	c	k	
k	n	o	c	k		

Answer: A clock.

page 98

Show What You Know!
lock, dock, rock, flock, shock

Write It!: Answers will vary.

page 99

Fill in the Blank
jump, stump, lump, grump

Word Puzzle

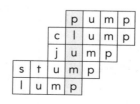

		p	u	m	p
	c	l	u	m	p
		j	u	m	p
s	t	u	m	p	
l	u	m	p		

Answer: Plump.

page 100

Show What You Know!
lump, pump, thump, hump, grump

Write It!: Answers will vary.

page 101

Fill in the Blank
reread, rewrite, rebuild, replay, reset

page 102

Show What You Know!
resweep, rewash, remake, restack, rewrite

Write It!: Answers will vary.

page 103

Fill in the Blank
unzip, unwell, unafraid, uneven, undress

page 104

Show What You Know!
unkind, unable, unsure, unwell, untrue

Write It!: Answers will vary.

page 105

Fill in the Blank
walked, picked, reached, painted, washed

page 106

Show What You Know!
washed, mixed, pressed, filled, cooked

Write It!: Answers will vary.

page 107

Fill in the Blank
drawing, reading, drinking, sleeping, jumping

page 108

Show What You Know!
flying, howling, chirping, blowing, swaying

Write It!: Answers will vary.